WORLD BANK STAFF WORKING PAPERS
Number 581

MANAGEMENT AND DEVELOPMENT SERIES
Number 8

Decentralization in Developing Countries

A Review of Recent Experience

Dennis A. Rondinelli
John R. Nellis
G. Shabbir Cheema

The World Bank
Washington, D.C., U.S.A.

Copyright © 1984
The International Bank for Reconstruction
and Development / THE WORLD BANK
1818 H Street, N.W.
Washington, D.C. 20433, U.S.A.

First printing January 1984
All rights reserved
Manufactured in the United States of America

This is a working document published informally by the World Bank. To present the results of research with the least possible delay, the typescript has not been prepared in accordance with the procedures appropriate to formal printed texts, and the World Bank accepts no responsibility for errors. The publication is supplied at a token charge to defray part of the cost of manufacture and distribution.

The views and interpretations in this document are those of the author(s) and should not be attributed to the World Bank, to its affiliated organizations, or to any individual acting on their behalf. Any maps used have been prepared solely for the convenience of the readers; the denominations used and the boundaries shown do not imply, on the part of the World Bank and its affiliates, any judgment on the legal status of any territory or any endorsement or acceptance of such boundaries.

The full range of World Bank publications is described in the *Catalog of World Bank Publications;* the continuing research program of the Bank is outlined in *World Bank Research Program: Abstracts of Current Studies.* Both booklets are updated annually; the most recent edition of each is available without charge from the Publications Distribution Unit of the Bank in Washington or from the European Office of the Bank, 66, avenue d'Iéna, 75116 Paris, France.

John R. Nellis and Dennis A. Rondinelli are professors at the Maxwell Graduate School of Citizenship and Public Affairs, Syracuse University, New York; G. Shabbir Cheema is development administration planner at the United Nations Center for Regional Development, Nagoya, Japan.

Library of Congress Cataloging in Publication Data

```
Rondinelli, Dennis A.
   Decentralization in developing countries.

   (World Bank staff working papers ; no. 581.
Management and development subseries ; no. 8)
    Bibliography: p.
    1. Developing countries--Politics and government.
2. Decentralization in government--Developing countries.
I. Nellis, John R.  II. Cheema, G. Shabbir.  III. Title.
IV. Series: World Bank staff working papers ; no. 581.
V. Series: World Bank staff working papers. Management
and development subseries ; no. 8)
JF60.R66  1983      351.007'3'091724       83-14712
ISBN 0-8213-0235-3
```

Abstract

A large number of governments in developing countries have attempted to decentralize development planning and management responsibilities during the past decade. Decentralization has taken a number of forms--deconcentration of functions within the central bureaucracy, delegation of semiautonomous or quasi-public corporations, devolution to local governments, and the transfer of functions to nongovernment organizations. The results have been mixed. In some countries decentralization has resulted in greater participation in development activities, more effective and efficient administration of local and rural development programs, and expanded administrative capacity outside of the national capital. But in nearly all countries where governments have attempted to decentralize, they have faced serious problems of implementation. Some problems arose from insufficient central political and bureaucratic support and others from ingrained centrist attitudes and behavior on the part of political and administrative leaders. In some countries, decentralization policies and programs were inappropriately designed, organized, and carried out. Nearly everywhere it was tried, decentralization was weakened by the failure to transfer sufficient financial resources to those organizations to which responsibilities were shifted.

If decentralization is viewed as an incremental process of institutional capacity-building, many of the experiments of the past decade can be judged as moderately successful. However, success depends heavily on careful planning and implementation. The most successful cases seem to be those in which the programs of decentralization were small in scope, were given adequate time to prove themselves, were centered around specific financial or managerial functions, and included a training component. In most developing countries, decentralization must be an incremental process of building the capacity of nongovernmental and local organizations to accept and carry out effectively new functions and responsibilities. The process must be carefully nurtured from the center and accompanied by a shift in the orientation of central bureaucracy from control to facilitation and support.

Acknowledgements

The authors are grateful for comments on an earlier version of the manuscript from Geoff Lamb, David Leonard, and William Siffin.

Papers in the Management and Development Series

Agarwala, Ramgopal. *Price Distortions and Growth in Developing Countries.* World Bank Staff Working Paper no. 575.

Agarwala, Ramgopal. *Planning in Developing Countries: Lessons of Experience.* World Bank Staff Working Paper no. 576.

Cochrane, Glynn. *Policies for Strengthening Local Government in Developing Countries.* World Bank Staff Working Paper no. 582.

Gordon, David. *Development Finance Companies, State and Privately Owned: A Review.* World Bank Staff Working Paper no. 578.

Gould, David J., and Jose A. Amaro-Reyes. *The Effects of Corruption on Administrative Performance: Illustrations from Developing Countries.* World Bank Staff Working Paper no. 580.

Knight, Peter T. *Economic Reform in Socialist Countries: The Experiences of China, Hungary, Romania, and Yugoslavia.* World Bank Staff Working Paper no. 579.

Kubr, Milan, and John Wallace. *Successes and Failures in Meeting the Management Challenge: Strategies and Their Implementation.* World Bank Staff Working Paper no. 585.

Lethem, Francis J., and Lauren Cooper. *Managing Project-Related Technical Assistance: The Lessons of Success.* World Bank Staff Working Paper no. 586.

Ozgediz, Selcuk. *Managing the Public Service in Developing Countries: Issues and Prospects.* World Bank Staff Working Paper no. 583.

Paul, Samuel. *Training for Public Administration and Management in Developing Countries: A Review.* World Bank Staff Working Paper no. 584.

Rondinelli, Dennis A., John R. Nellis, and G. Shabbir Cheema. *Decentralization in Developing Countries: A Review of Recent Experience.* World Bank Staff Working Paper no. 581.

Shinohara, Miyohei, Toru Yanagihara, and Kwang Suk Kim. *The Japanese and Korean Experiences in Managing Development.* Ed. Ramgopal Agarwala. World Bank Staff Working Paper no. 574.

Shirley, Mary M. *Managing State-Owned Enterprises.* World Bank Staff Working Paper no. 577.

Foreword

This study is one in a series of World Bank Staff Working Papers devoted to issues of development management. Prepared as background papers for the World Development Report 1983, they provide an in-depth treatment of the subjects dealt with in Part II of the Report. The thirteen papers cover topics ranging from comprehensive surveys of management issues in different types of public sector institutions (for example, state-owned enterprises, the public service, and local government agencies) to broad overviews of such subjects as planning, management training, technical assistance, corruption, and decentralization.

The central concern underlying these papers is the search for greater efficiency in setting and pursuing development goals. The papers focus on the role of the state in this process, stress the importance of appropriate incentives, and assess the effectiveness of alternative institutional arrangements. They offer no general prescriptions, as the developing countries are too diverse--politically, culturally, and in economic resources--to allow the definition of a single strategy.

The papers draw extensively on the experiences of the World Bank and other international agencies. They were reviewed by a wide range of readership from developing and developed countries inside and outside the Bank. They were edited by Victoria Macintyre. Rhoda Blade-Charest, Banjonglak Duangrat, Jaunianne Fawkes, and Carlina Jones prepared the manuscripts for publication.

I hope that these studies will be useful to practitioners and academicians of development management around the world.

Pierre Landell-Mills
Staff Director
World Development Report 1983

CONTENTS

		Page
I.	Introduction	1
II.	Objectives of Decentralization	5
III.	Types of Decentralization	13
	Deconcentration	10
	Delegation	15
	Devolution	19
	Privatization	23
IV.	Assessing the Results of Decentralization	27
	The Mixed Results of Decentralization Policies	30
	Decentralization as an Incremental Process of Capacity Building	41
V.	Conditions and Factors Affecting the Implementation of Decentralization	46
	Degree of Political Commitment and Administrative Support	47
	Attitudinal, Behavioral, and Cultural Conditions Conducive to Decentralization	51
	Effective Design and Organization of Decentralization Programs	57
	Adequate Financial, Human, and Physical Resources	63
VI.	Conclusions and Implications	69
Annex 1.	Donor Assisted Decentralization: Indonesia's Provincial Development Program	76
Annex 2.	China: The "Production Responsibility" System	80
Annex 3.	Deconcentration: The Programme de Developpement Rural in Tunisia	86
References		88

Acronyms

FAMA	Federal Agricultural Marketing Authority (Malaysia)
FEC	Fonds d'Equipment Communal (Morocco)
IRDP	Integrated Rural Development Program (Pakistan)
PDAP	Provincial Development Assistance Program (Philippines)
PDP	Provincial Development Program (Indonesia)
PDR	Programme de Developpment Rural (Tunisia)
REG	Rural Employment Generation (Thailand)
SFDA	Small Farmers Development Agency (India)

I. Introduction

Developing countries have generally regarded unified, centralized, and regulatory government as highly desirable. Centralization has tended to be both the norm and the ideal that pervades concepts of political, economic, and administrative organization in the Third World. It is not difficult to understand why this is the case. In most countries that were formerly colonies, centralized political and administrative institutions were a direct legacy of the colonial rulers, and until recently these systems were largely left untouched, or were further centralized.

Centralized economic planning, intervention, and control have been viewed by national government authorities as the correct path to follow, despite frequent and increasingly detailed accounts of their negative effects. A widely held suspicion in the Third World is that the principal mechanism of economic decentralization--the market--is immoral and anarchic, and that its impersonal operation rewards the few at the expense of the many. Many neoclassical economists would agree that markets in developing countries work imperfectly. But most would conclude that the proper solution to this problem is to find ways of removing obstacles in order to allow the market to operate more freely.

Many Third World intellectuals and policymakers have a different interpretation: they believe market imperfections justify continuing central control and intervention. This is not simply an economic debate; there are powerful political reasons for maintaining central control and intervention. Many political leaders emphasize the primacy of the public sector, which provides positions in the civil service and parastatal institutions with which to reward loyal political followers. They keep under central government control those factors--such as wages, prices, tariffs, food subsidies, and import and export regulations--that are considered to be most important for maintaining political stability. Clearly, policies promoting centralization usually pay off, at least in the short run, in material and political returns for the dominant elites. As long as economic centralization reinforces centralized political control, it will have strong supporters--who usually appeal to the need for national unity--despite the most persuasive rationalistic economic criticisms. Thus, throughout the discussion of administrative reorganization that follows, it should be remembered that attempts to counter centralization are intensely political activities; they inevitably produce political consequences.

Despite these pressures for increasing centralization, a large number of developing countries that are politically, economically, and ideologically diverse began decentralizing some development planning and management functions during the 1970s and early 1980s. They did so because of dissatisfaction with the results of national planning and administration, and because the underlying rationale of international development strategies changed during the 1970s. The goal of development policies in most countries was to distribute the benefits of economic growth more equitably to increase the productivity and income of all segments of society, and to raise the living standards of the poor. But because policymakers found it difficult to formulate and implement these strategies entirely from the center, they sought new ways of eliciting greater participation in development planning and administration. Moreover, by the end of the 1970s, most developing countries were facing severe financial problems, decreasing levels of exports, rising prices for energy and imported goods, and diminishing foreign assistance. Because of all of these factors, governments became interested in finding ways of using limited resources more effectively. Decentralization appeared to be at least a partial solution to their growing problems.

Many governments in Third World countries had become more centralized during the 1950s and early 1960s, after receiving independence from colonial regimes. They, naturally, first turned their attention to nation-building and thus invested heavily in programs for economic development. Both processes seemed to require and legitimize centralized management. But, over time, the modest and sometimes negative consequences of central planning and administration became apparent. A ministry of agriculture that applies crop production quotas to all areas of the country without taking regional variations in soil and climate conditions into account, for example, hinders production and wastes resources. When central planners design rural development projects in the national capital without thoroughly understanding local social, economic, physical, and organization conditions, they often generate opposition among local groups or encounter such apathy that the projects are doomed to failure at the outset. Overworked and cautious central finance officers, who typically are responsible for approving even petty expenditures for local development projects, often release funds for agricultural projects so late in the fiscal year that optimal planting times are missed. The inability of project managers to receive resources from the central government in a timely manner--because of the need for approval by multiple levels of higher administration--delays implementation and causes serious cost overruns. Central administrators cannot know the complex variety of factors that affect the success of projects in local communities throughout the country. In their attempt to cope with this uncertainty, they create highly centralized and standardized procedures; or, through fear of making mistakes, they do nothing about urgent decisions that are essential for implementing local projects and programs. Excessive centralization is viewed as the cause of poor performance; decentralization of one form or another as the corrective device.

This study reviews a variety of recent experiences with decentralization in a large number of developing countries. The review indicates that, to date, no one has demonstrated conclusively that decentralization actually solves the problems noted earlier, or that it is necessarily more cost-effective than centralization. The study shows that decentralization is not a "quick fix" for the management problems of developing countries. The factors that make it such an attractive policy are usually the same ones that make it difficult to implement. In general, we found little evidence to contest the conclusions of a United Nations (1982, p. 6) assessment that "the actual impact of decentralization for effective administration has been very limited."

Nonetheless, we believe that guarded optimism on the utility of decentralization in developing countries is justified. This conclusion is warranted by the number of cases in which small but clear-cut improvements have occurred as the result of decentralization programs. Indonesia's Provincial Development Program, Morocco's local government reform, efforts to decentralize in Thailand, Pakistan, and Tunisia, and other cases, show perceptible improvements in resource distribution, local participation, extension of public services to rural areas, project identification and implementation, and employment generation.

This study describes these and other programs, examines their results, and identifies the factors affecting their implementation. It concludes by offering operational guidelines for designing and implementing future decentralization programs. The recommendations are mainly cautionary. We suggest, for example, beginning in a small way and expanding only carefully and incrementally, realizing at the outset that progressive change will take a long time to achieve. We suggest that decentralization places special and continuing demands on central as well as local officials. None of these conclusions are surprising revelations, but they yield what we believe are basic principles for improving policy formulation and implementation.

II. Objectives of Decentralization

The extraordinary scope of the concept of decentralization is revealed by the many objectives that it supposedly serves. An often expressed hope is that decentralization will reduce overload and congestion in the channels of administration and communication. Programs are decentralized with the expectation that delays will be reduced and that administrators' indifference to satisfying the needs of their clientele will be overcome. It is thought that decentralization will improve government's responsiveness to the public and increase the quantity and quality of the services it provides.

Decentralization is often justified as a way of managing national economic development more effectively or efficiently. But it is obvious that governments in developing countries that have tried to decentralize during the 1970s and 1980s have not always had effectiveness or efficiency as their primary goals. They have rarely embarked on a course of decentralization primarily for economic reasons. Indeed, the economic impacts of decentralization have not usually been calculated beforehand. Thus, recent experiments with decentralization cannot be assessed entirely by economic criteria. In many countries decentralization is pursued in reaction to the technical failures of comprehensive national development planning or the weak impact of multisectoral, macroeconomic development programming. Neither of these have significantly increased the ability of central governments to formulate, articulate, and implement national development policies (Rondinelli 1978). Decentralization is often seen as a way of increasing the ability of central government officials to obtain better and less suspect information about local or regional conditions, to plan local programs more responsively, and to react more quickly to unanticipated problems that inevitably arise during implementation (Maddick 1963). In theory, decentralization should allow projects to be completed sooner by giving local managers greater discretion in decisionmaking so as to enable them to cut through the "red tape" and the ponderous procedures often associated with overcentralized administrations (Rondinelli 1981a).

In some countries, decentralization is seen as a way of mobilizing support for national development policies by making them better known at the local level. Local governments or administrative units, it is assumed, can be effective channels of communication between the national government and local communities. Greater participation in development planning and management supposedly promotes national unity by giving groups in different regions in a country a greater ability to participate in planning and decisionmaking, and thus increases their stake in maintaining political stability. Greater equity in the allocation of government resouces for investment is presumed more likely when representatives of a wide variety of political, religious, ethnic, and social groups participate in development decisionmaking (Uphoff and Esman 1974; Esman and Montgomery 1982).

In countries where administrative capacity is low, decentralization is sometimes seen as a means of creating larger numbers of skilled administrators and managers. Such skills, it is argued, are only strengthened when administrators have meaningful managerial responsibilities. Centralization concentrates experience in the national capital, and contributes little to developing local leadership and initiative (USAID 1979a). Studies of decentralization of land reform administration in the late 1960s and early 1970s concluded that, properly carried out, decentralization increased officials' knowledge of local conditions, motivated community leaders to take an active role, created better communications between local residents and leaders and between local and national officials, and increased community solidarity and interest in land reform projects (Montgomery 1972).

Moreover, it has become clear that many functions that are currently the responsibility of central ministries or agencies are performed poorly because of the difficulty of extending central services to local communities. Maintenance of roads, irrigation channels and equipment, and other basic physical infrastructure is sometimes done better by local governments or administrative units--when they are given adequate funds and technical assistance--than by central agencies, which cannot easily monitor deterioration or breakdowns. Indeed, for some activities, decentralization could increase the efficiency of central ministries by relieving top management of routine, repetitive tasks and allowing them more time to plan and monitor programs that absolutely require central direction or control. Subnational administrations can, it is argued, be more effective levels at which to coordinate actions requiring the participation of many agencies.

Little research has been done on the socioeconomic, political, or physical correlates of decentralization, and thus little is known about which factors are associated with government pressures to deconcentrate or devolve planning and administrative responsibilities. Vieira's (1967) study of forty-five countries, undertaken during the mid-1960s, indicates that the degree of devolution (measured by the ratio of local government revenues and expenditures to total government spending and receipts over a ten-year period) in both Western and Third World countries was significantly correlated with five factors: (1) the age of the nation--older, well-established national governments having a higher degree of devolution than newer ones; (2) the size of gross national product--those countries with high levels of GNP tended to have higher degrees of devolution than poorer countries; (3) the level of development of the mass media--those countries with a more sophisticated and widespread mass communications system tended to be more decentralized than those with incipient or weak systems; (4) the level of industrialization-- industrialized countries tended to be more decentralized than those with agricultural economies; and (5) the number of local governments. The size and density of population and the physical size of the country were not significant. Nor was the level of urbanization. Constitutional structure and ethnic composition of the population were also insignificant factors. Sherwood (1969, p. 75) concluded from this and other studies that the strong association between devolution and economic and technological factors "tends to validate the generally held position that diverse structures within a system can be tolerated only when the integrity of the system itself is not in question. That is, national unity seems to be a necesary precondition for devolution."

Ultimately, however, decentralization is an ideological principle, associated with objectives of self-reliance, democratic decisionmaking, popular participation in government, and accountability of public officials to citizens. As such, it has been pursued as a desirable political objective in itself.

Although developing country governments have offered a wide range of justifications for decentralizing, the results have been mixed. Third World governments have faced myriad problems in designing and implementing programs for decentralizing development administration. Even where the programs have been relatively successful, not all of the anticipated benefits have accrued to either central or local administrative units (Cheema and Rondinelli 1983). Ultimately, decentralization is a political decision, and its implementation a reflection of a country's political process.

The following sections review decentralization efforts that have been tried in developing countries since the early 1970s, assess the results, describe the basic conditions that affect their implementation, and offer a set of general operational principles to guide governments that are considering decentralization of development planning and management.

III. Types of Decentralization

The concept of decentralization is broad; its component parts are many. Definitions and classifications are therefore necessary. Decentralization can be defined as the transfer of responsibility for planning, management and resource raising and allocation from the central government and its agencies to: (a) field units of central government ministries or agencies, (b) subordinate units or levels of government, (c) semiautonomous public authorities or corporations, (d) areawide, regional or functional authorities, or (e) nongovernmental private or voluntary organizations (Rondinelli 1981a).

Decentralization can be broad or constrained in scope. The degree of responsibility for and discretion in decisionmaking that is transferred by the central government can vary, from simply adjusting workloads within central government organizations, to the divesting of all government responsibilities for performing a set of what were previously considered to be public sector functions. This evident complexity makes it necessary to distinguish among the major types of decentralization that have been tried in developing countries. They can be categorized into four types: <u>deconcentration, delegation, devolution,</u> and <u>privatization</u> (Rondinelli 1981a). Some governments have used all four types, simultaneously or at different times. Some began with one approach and later shifted to another after assessing initial results. Other governments have used various combinations of the four. A number of countries have devolved development management responsibilities to local governments but have maintained strong indirect controls over them. Privatization has usually evolved from situations in which private sector firms began offering goods and services that government provided poorly, or not at all, or only in some parts of the country, rather than from deliberate efforts by governments to divest themselves of public functions.

<u>Deconcentration</u>

Deconcentration is the handing over of some amount of administrative authority or responsibility to lower levels within central government ministries and agencies. It is a shifting of the workload from centrally located officials to staff or offices outside of the national capital. Deconcentration, when it is more than mere reorganization, gives some discretion to field agents to plan and implement programs and projects, or to adjust central directives to local conditions, within guidelines set by central ministry or agency headquarters.

Deconcentration has been the most frequently used form of decentralization in developing countries since the early 1970s. In Indonesia, Morocco, Pakistan, the Philippines, Sri Lanka, Thailand, Tunisia, and elsewhere, deconcentration has been encouraged through financial grants from the central governments to provincial, district, or local administrative units. Other governments have deconcentrated operations by creating coordinating units at the subnational level or through incentives or contract arrangements. In Thailand, from 1979 to 1982, a percentage of the national budget was set aside to allow provincial governments to assist <u>tambon</u> (village) councils to identify, formulate, and implement small-scale, employment-generating projects that furthered the national government's objectives of increasing agricultural production and household income in drought-prone areas (Noranitipadungkarn 1982). In Indonesia, the central government provides resources from foreign assistance funds and from the national budget, through the Provincial Development Program. This arrangement enables provincial and local planning units to undertake programs and projects for increasing productivity and incomes in rural areas (MacAndrews, Sibero, and Fisher 1981; see Annex 1).

Similarly, the central government in Pakistan has created and supervises <u>markaz</u> councils to integrate and coordinate the agricultural, credit, public works, marketing, and infrastructure development activities of central government ministries with those of local agricultural cooperatives and private sector firms. The Philippines, with the assistance of the U.S. Agency for International Development, provides technical, financial, and management assistance through the Provincial Development Assistance Program (PDAP)--supervised by the Ministry of Local Government and Community Development--to provincial governors. The program aims at building a provincial development staff. The idea is to assist the governor in identifying development needs, formulating project proposals for funding by national ministries, mobilizing local resources to finance provincial development programs, and supervising and managing the projects that are ultimately funded. The Philippines has also deconcentrated by creating regional development councils and planning staffs as subordinate units of the National Economic and Development Authority. Regional planning organizations attempt to translate national development goals into provincial and local projects, and to coordinate the activities of national ministries and agencies within the region (Landau 1980; Iglesias 1977).

In Sri Lanka, prior to 1980, deconcentration took the form of district development councils. Coordinating committees were established under the direction of the government agent. The local member of parliament played an important intermediary role in reconciling and integrating the local development activities of national departments and agencies (Wanasinghe 1982).

In 1979, China began to deconcentrate: much of the responsibility for agricultural production decisions, work arrangements, and distribution of the proceeds of communal enterprise was handed over to production teams and management committees. This Production Responsibility System allows small groups, and even individuals, to choose between methods for payment, either by meeting production quotas set by higher level authorities, or according to agricultural yields within the production team. Under the latter, increased production means increased income. More discretion has been given to production teams in establishing and managing the relationship between collective and sideline household production. Farmers now have a voice in choosing the type of work responsibility system adopted by the communes (see Annex 2). The purpose of the reforms was to shift the emphasis of national development policy from promoting equality in the distribution of income--a goal that has largely been accomplished in rural China--to increasing agricultural productivity and raising the standard of living. Deconcentration through contractual arrangements supposedly allows communes to implement the governing principle of the collective economy in China: "from each according to his ability, to each according to his work" (Gengou 1982).

The governments of Libya, Algeria, Tunisia, and Morocco all claim to have embarked on a process of putting power and responsiblity into the hands of "the people" in their countries. The claim is that democratically elected, representative local institutions have been or are being given jurisdiction over issues formerly controlled solely by central decisionmakers. To back up the claim, all four governments point to various tasks, the regulation of which has been transferred from national bureaucrats to local councils, or at least to local officials. In the previously French North African states, the claim is buttressed by the assignment of cadres to supporting civil service positions in the local government system, and by efforts to create training schools and special services for local government administrators (who will, however, continue to be central government employees). In Morocco, the government has gone even further in deconcentrating development management. It is requiring that communal councils be consulted by central authorities when any action of local concern is under consideration. Communal councils eventually will take over the responsibility for all local social services and become the centers of local development planning. Communes can now apply to several capital funding sources for both recurring and developmental financing. Locally generated and managed projects for education and training, roads, public health, physical infrastructure, agriculture, housing and communications can be financed from loans and grants from the Communal Supply

Fund, the Local Authorities Development Fund, and the Special Regional Development Fund (Nellis 1983a).

In Tunisia, each of the country's twenty gouvernorats receive an annual grant from the central government to formulate and carry out local employment generation and development projects. These must be reviewed and approved by the central Ministry of Plan before the money can be spent (see Annex 3). The entire civil service in Libya has been reassigned to locally based popular committees. These, supposedly, are directed and fully supervised by a representative Basic Popular Congress. In Algeria, Morocco, and Tunisia the general term used to encompass these efforts at democratization, localization, and participation is decentralization; the processes in Libya are part of the notion of jamahiriya (Nellis 1983a).

Among the most notable experiments in deconcentration in East Africa have been those in Kenya and Tanzania. In 1972, the government of Tanzania abolished traditional local governments, absorbed local officers into the national civil service, decentralized national ministries, and attempted to consolidate the rural population into ujamaa villages that could be efficiently provided with services and facilities. Although there is some debate among scholars over the issue of whether or not ujamaa was intended to be a decentralization program, it manifests many of the characteristics of deconcentration, and is described as such here. In Kenya, at roughly the same time, provincial and district development advisory committees were established. They aimed to stimulate development at the local level by involving in the planning process not only government officials but also popularly elected representatives (Rondinelli 1980).

In each instance, the distinguishing characteristic of deconcentration has been that the authority of responsibility for specific functions has been shifted by the central government to a lower level of administration, but one that remains within the central government structure.

Delegation

Delegation transfers managerial responsibility for specifically defined functions to organizations that are outside the regular bureaucratic structure and that are only indirectly controlled by the central government. Delegation has long been used in administrative law. It implies that a sovereign authority creates or transfers to an agent specified functions and duties, which the agent has broad discretion to carry out. However, ultimate responsibility remains with the sovereign authority. In developing countries, responsibilities have been delegated to public corporations, regional development agencies, special function authorities, semiautonomous project implementation units, and a variety of parastatal organizations (Rondinelli 1981a).

In some countries, delegation is looked upon as a way of removing important functions from inefficient government bureaucracies. In others, it has been viewed as a way for government indirectly to provide goods and services for which user or unit charges can be made, but which are not effectively provided by the civil service. Some countries have used delegation as a means of maintaining public control over highly profitable or valuable resources. It is assumed that autonomy or semiautonomy will free the organizations to which functions are delegated from the cumbersome or patronage-ridden personnel regulations, rigid and incentiveless bureaucratic pay scales, and unproductive work habits frequently found in the regular civil service. Moreover, delegation is seen as a way of offering public goods and services through a more "business-like" organizational structure that makes use of managerial and accounting techniques normally associated with private enterprise. Many international assistance agencies have created semi-autonomous public authorities to implement their projects so that loans and grants might be kept separate from the normal central government budgeting and accounting process. The idea is that an "audit trail" can be established for the expenditure of foreign aid funds so that they will not be "co-mingled" with national financial resources. International donors have wanted their projects to be "quarantined," not simply to protect them from the inefficiency of the civil service, but to make them more visible. This arrangement makes the projects easier to evaluate and allows "show-cases" to be created through which follow-on funding can be more readily generated. Moreover, special authorities or public corporations are often set up to create clear lines of command within the organization, to ensure direct responsibility for managerial performance, and to provide an environment conducive to flexible and demand-oriented management (Boodhoo 1976; Cheema 1982).

Delegation has been used extensively. In East Africa, public corporations and special authorities have been used to finance, construct, and manage physical infrastructure projects such as highways, dams, hydroelectric facilities, railroads, and transportation systems, and to organize and manage large-scale agricultural activities such as cotton growing in the Sudan and tea raising in Kenya (King 1967; Khalil 1970). In Latin America, governments have delegated a wide range of functions--from the production of essential inputs for industrialization through the management of industrial enterprises, to the provision of social services--to public authorities. Mexico has made extensive use of public corporations, state marketing boards, and "mixed enterprises," which combine state and private capital for investment in high priority development ventures. The government has also established credit and loan institutions, state holding companies, regional development commissions, and social service institutes. Those that run businesses—banks, hotels, steel mills, airlines, railroads, television stations, and telephone services, for example—are called <u>parastate enterprises</u>. They operate under commercial law, but have government representatives on their boards of directors. They are subject to federal government regulation. Those that provide social services—health, education, social security benefits—are called <u>decentralized organizations,</u> and are structured as institutes or councils with their own governing boards, sources of funding, property, and legal status. These organizations are governed by federal administrative law (Harris 1983).

The government of Mexico delegates a wide variety of functions to independent commissions and councils, which oversee or manage special functions. These include the development of arid agricultural areas, setting electrical rates, and promoting tourism. At the beginning of the 1980s there were over 800 independent councils and commissions, 100 decentralized organizations, and 400 <u>parastate enterprises</u> in Mexico (Harris 1983; Graham 1980).

A similar sort of delegation has been used in Brazil, where public enterprises and mixed enterprises and societies account for almost half of the liquid capital invested. The larger and more important they are, the greater their degree of political and administrative independence.

A number of developing countries have tended to delegate control over the exploitation, processing, and exportation of valuable natural resources such as minerals and petroleum to publicly owned corporations and special authorities, rather than allow either private enterprise or the normal civil service to take responsibility for them. SONATRACH in Algeria, Petroleos Mexicanos (PEMEX) in Mexico, COMIBOL in Bolivia, PETROBRAS in Brazil, and PERTAMINA in Indonesia have all played an important role in the petroleum and mining industries in those countries. Governments have chosen to delegate management of these functions to special authorities because the regular bureaucracy was considered incapable of regulating or controlling such activities, and its direct management of them was said to be inappropriate.

Indonesia made extensive use of public enterprises during the 1950s and 1960s. As one observer noted, "by proliferating state corporations throughout the economy, each enterprise having exclusive jurisdiction over a key sector, it was hoped that economic development would unfold with unparalleled rapidity" (Fabrikant 1975). Delegation of important economic functions to public corporations was also motivated by the government's desire to nationalize and control critical elements of the economy that had previously been under the influence of foreign investors and multinational corporations. It was further motivated by the government's desire to reduce the influence of the overseas Chinese business community in the economy.

Indeed, delegation has frequently been used in some countries as a means of promoting high priority development objectives that seemingly could not be achieved by either the private sector or the national bureaucracy. The task of improving the access of poor Malay farmers to agricultural markets was delegated to the Federal Agricultural Marketing Authority (FAMA) in Malaysia, for example, because the central government could not control the markets directly, and the private sector was dominated by an ethnic group that was not organized for or interested in serving indigenous smallholders. FAMA was given the tasks of establishing marketing, processing, and grading centers; expanding markets for agricultural products of smallholders, and purchasing from and selling the goods of all poor farmers who had difficulty marketing them (Nor Ghani 1982). Similarly, when India faced severe food crises during the 1960s, the government turned to semiautonomous project units to carry out integrated rural development programs. When it became clear that poor farmers were not benefiting proportionately from the Green Revolution during the 1970s, the government established the Small Farmers Development Agency (SFDA) to provide subsidized credit in rural areas in an attempt to reduce the growing income disparities between large- and small-scale cultivators. Organized as semiautonomous registered societies at the district level, the SFDA was created because central government leaders believed that local governments were not strong enough to carry out participative development activities on their own. Here, as in many other instances, the national civil service was said to be too unresponsive and inflexible to manage such a program creatively (Mathur 1982).

Other countries have delegated high priority development programs to multifunctional authorities or commissions. Unlike a public corporation, which is intended both to execute projects and manage them after completion, multipurpose authorities are more often established simply to initiate projects that are later turned over to other organizations to operate. They are usually created to expedite essential development tasks or to initiate politically sensitive activities. They are often considered "temporary" organizations that will be phased out of existence when their objectives are attained.

Devolution

Devolution is the creation or strengthening--financially or legally--of subnational units of government, the activities of which are substantially outside the direct control of the central government. Under devolution, local units of government are autonomous and independent, and their a legal status makes them separate or distinct from the central government. Central authorities frequently exercise only indirect, supervisory control over such units. Normally, local governments have clear and legally recognized geographical boundaries within which they exercise an exclusive authority to perform explicitly granted or reserved functions. They have corporate or statutory authority to raise revenues and make expenditures. They should be perceived by local citizens as organizations providing services that satisfy their needs, and as governmental units over which they have some influence. Devolution establishes reciprocal and mutually benefiting relationships between central and local governments. That is, the local governments are not merely subordinate administrative units, but they have the ability to interact reciprocally with other units of government in the political system of which they are a part. In most developing countries where devolution has been tried, the local governments have met some of these criteria (Sherwood 1969).

Central governments have devolved development planning and management activities for a number of reasons. In some countries, the intention was to place the mechanisms of governance much closer to, or in direct contact with, the citizenry. The idea was to reduce the levels of administration through which activities had to pass, and to enhance citizenry productivity and participation by increasing their involvement in development activities. In other cases, local governments were assigned functions that were considered to be predominatly or entirely local in nature or that were difficult to manage from the center. In Algeria, for example, elected communal popular assemblies were handed the task of designating beneficiaries of the land reform process, partly because these bodies had the necessary local knowledge, and partly because the central authorities considered the issue too hot to handle. In still other countries, devolution resulted from the demands of ethnic or regional groups for greater autonomy or self-governance, or from the inability of the central government to resolve regional or local tensions.

Relatively few developing countries have decentralized through devolution during the past two decades. Those making the attempt have transferred quite a broad range of activities to local governments. One of the most extensive attempts at devolution has been in the Sudan. There, provincial councils and provincial commissioners have been given the responsibility for nearly all public functions except national security, posts and communications, foreign affairs, banking, and the judiciary. These were reserved to the central government. The country has been divided into administrative regions, each with a governor and regional assembly that have semiautonomous legislative and executive responsibilities. Provincial governments have the power to impose local taxes and fees, maintain law and order, finance public projects, prepare annual budgets, recommend development projects to central government agencies, and establish and administer self-financing development activities. They oversee all the work of central ministries and government departments within the province. Devolution was undertaken to shift responsibility for local services to localities and to provide broader participation in development planning and management in a country of huge physical size, in which it is difficult or impossible to provide services efficiently to all regions from the national capital. The crucial goal, however, was to find a way of ending the civil war and to increase the commitment of heterogenous religious, ethnic, and tribal groups to nation building by giving them a larger part in governance (Rondinelli 1981a).

For many of the same reasons, and because of demands for greater autonomy by political interests in one region that contained the nation's most productive export enterprises, Papua New Guinea, between 1976 and 1978 devolved to provincial governments full legislative and management responsibilities for a wide range of local functions, and considerable responsibility for others that were "concurrent" local-national functions. In each province an elected assembly and executive council, headed by a premier, was given control over a wide range of matters. Provincial governments can levy and collect taxes; in addition, they receive refunded revenues from licenses, fees, and royalties collected by the national government in the provinces, and a "derivative grant" equivalent to 1.25 percent of the value of export goods produced in the province. Moreover, provincial governments receive an annual unconditional grant from the national government to offset costs of administration of functions devolved to them. They use these mainly to construct and maintain public works. Conditional grants are also available for previously national functions--such as the operation of general hospitals--that are now managed by the provinces. Since 1979, sectoral programs in health and education have been added to provincial responsibilities (Conyers 1981; Conyers and Westcott 1979).

Similarly, Nigeria devolved a wide range of statutory local functions--such as maintenance of law and order; construction and maintenance of public roads and bridges; formulation and implementation of rural development schemes; agricultural development; and the provision of health, water, and housing--to local governments in 1976. Local governments then became the only legally recognized level of government below the state level. Some local council members are elected directly and others are appointed by state governors. Both the federal and state governments are required to make annual statutory grants from their budgets to local governments. Localities also have some powers to raise their own revenues, but these are limited (Idode 1980).

Privatization

Some governments have divested themselves of responsibility for functions and have either transferred them to voluntary organizations or allowed them to be performed by private enterprises. In some cases, governments have transferred responsibility to "parallel organizations" such as national industrial and trade associations, professional groups, religious organizations, political parties, or cooperatives. These parallel organizations have been given the responsibility to license, regulate, or supervise their members in performing functions that were previously performed or regulated by the government. In some cases, government may decentralize by shifting the responsibility for producing goods and supplying services that were previously offered by parastatal or public corporations to privately owned or controlled enterprises. More often, government transfers responsibilities to organizations that represent various interests in society and that are established and operated by members of those organizations. These include farmers' cooperatives, credit associations, mutual aid societies, village development organizations, trade unions, or women's and youth clubs. Moreover, decentralization may be implicit in the concept of "debureaucratization"; that is, decisions are allowed to be made through political processes that involve larger numbers of special interest groups, rather than exclusively or primarily by government through legislation, executive degree, or administrative regulation (Ralston, Anderson, and Colson 1981; Friedman 1983).

Voluntary organizations in Sri Lanka, for example, have come to play an important role in delivering services to meet basic human needs. They run day-care centers, nursery schools, health clinics, homes for destitute children, and old age homes; and they provide vocational training, nonformal education, and sports and recreation programs. They operate rural development projects and community self-help programs that provide social overhead capital--roads, water tanks, irrigation canals, sanitation facilities, and wells. Many provide working capital for local, small-scale agricultural and handicraft projects and market outlets for the goods produced in villages (James 1982). These private groups either supplement or exclusively provide services offered in many other countries through government agencies.

Cooperative organizations in other Asian countries provide a channel for the private participation of local residents in community development projects, help mobilize local resources, channel information about local conditions and needs to government officials, and provide a wide range of productive and social services to their members (Cheema 1983). In Bangladesh, cooperatives are primary sources of credit for poor farmers, supplementing the capital borrowed by farmers through the private market. Cooperatives in Egypt provide farmers with seeds, fertilizer, and credit, and maintain markets through which they can sell their produce. Similar functions are performed by cooperative organizations and private establishments in Indonesia, Malaysia, the Philippines, and Sri Lanka (Uphoff and Esman 1974). In most of these instances, governments continue to exercise some amount of supervision and support. At the margin, the distinction between privatization and delegation is blurred.

Controversial or experimental activities, which governments have been reluctant to sponsor or even to become directly involved in, have often been taken up by voluntary organizations. Family planning services, for instance, have been initiated by private voluntary organizations in most developing countries, sometimes with the tacit support of the government and sometimes with little or no government encouragement. Private family planning associations introduce the concept, test the market for services, provide information, and manage service delivery. In most cases they mobilize the support for family planning services, mother and child health care, and prenatal health services that are eventually provided by government (Cuca and Pierce 1977).

Voluntary and religious organizations have been heavily involved in providing basic health care in rural areas, where government health programs are often weak and private services are virtually nonexistent. The Salvation Army has operated village health clinics in Ghana for more than three decades, financing them from user fees and worldwide contributions. Catholic Relief Services, the Christian Medical Commission, and other religious groups supplement the services provided by government agencies in rural areas of India, Korea, and other Asian countries (American Public Health Association 1982).

In some situations, activities need to be undertaken that are simply beyond the capacity of any existing government agency. In these cases it is often impossible to build administrative or technical capability quickly within existing agencies, or to create new government organizations without external assistance. Thus, governments turn to indigenous or multinational corporations, or to foreign technical consultants. Governments in developing nations have used a number of private sector organizational arrangements for project implementation—they have encouraged foreign direct investment in high-priority or pioneering industries, created joint ventures with indigenous or multinational firms, contracted for technical assistance or consultant services, created "turnkey" construction agreements with private firms, and allowed private voluntary organizations to carry out projects alone or in conjunction with government agencies.

Encouraging foreign private firms to implement projects, as Streeten (1971) found, can generate significant benefits. It can result in the transfer of technology and skills essential for initiating new industries or modernizing a lagging sector of the economy. It can give local people opportunities to improve management and technical skills by working under the supervision of foreign managers and technicians. The operations of multinational firms are often observed and copied by domestic firms and government agencies, which thereby learn how to improve their own administrative, production, marketing, and distribution techniques. When backward and forward linkages are established with local industries, the operations of multinational companies can increase demand for local products and encourage higher standards of production. For government agencies, the advantages of subcontracting to, or working with, foreign companies, as Hallet (1971, p. 224) has pointed out, lie in the "economies in or sharing of risks, financial resources, management and personnel, corporate know-how and other intellectual property." Subcontracting increases the possibilities that projects for which local expertise is not abundant will be completed effectively and efficiently. The use of private firms can give governments greater flexibility in combining capital, technological experience, marketing and distribution processes, and production techniques in different ways for different types of projects. In some cases, joint ventures that provide government with partial brand ownership of internationally known products may create a new source of revenue. Such ventures can give governments new sources of equity capital, alternative means of securing and guaranteeing loans, and a way of sharing the risks of investment.

Thus, one can see that the concept of decentralization covers a wide range of activities and ideas.

IV. Assessing the Results of Decentralization

Despite its vast scope, decentralization has seldom, if ever, lived up to expectations. Regardless of its modest success rate, however, government planners, donor institutions, and observers of the development process continue to promote it. Why? Part of the reason is that decentralization often serves as an instrument for achieving political objectives. Thus, even though programs are usually justified on the basis of their potential for increasing administrative efficiency and effectiveness, they are frequently not assessed by their economic or administrative results, but rather by their political effects. Often, the rationale for decentralization is that it will increase political stability. Therefore, considerable deviation from principles of efficient management will be tolerated--perhaps even encouraged--by central and local administrative units, as long as political conditions remain quiescent and dominant community interests are served.

Another reason for the continued support of decentralization--in the absence of definitive proof that it promotes more efficient or effective administration--is that highly centralized procedures are manifestly ineffective in many countries, especially in implementing local development programs. Often, the proposed solution to such problems is simply to reverse things to the way they have been done in the past, rather than to deal with them directly. That is, some policymakers seek to solve problems indirectly by creating a more decentralized system. When poor performance continues in the initial stages, it is not attributed to the new structure, but to supposedly correctable difficulties in starting a new operation. Only if it becomes overwhelmingly clear that the opposite type of structure performs no better than the original will analysts seek to return to or modify the original arrangement. This situation may explain why cycles of centralization and decentralization have occurred in developing countries since the 1950s.

To these difficulties must be added the complexities of evaluating the impact of decentralization, which arise from the fact that it is primarily a political process that works through a number of nonpolitical channels. Each one of these channels, as we have shown, transfers a different amount or type of responsibility and power from the central government to other organizations. This means that in all decentralization programs one must deal not only with administrative and management issues, but also with some complicating factors, namely: (a) decentralization implies that actors and agencies possessing powers must willingly give them up, or be forced or persuaded to do so; and (b) decentralization programs almost always aim at much more than managerial reforms; they try to reduce the sociopolitical alienation of particular groups or regions. Moreover, different groups within developing countries advocate decentralization for very different reasons, some of which are inevitably conflicting.

It should be noted that centralization and decentralization are not mutually exclusive or dichotomous arrangements for governance. Few, if any, countries are either totally centralized or totally decentralized. Thus, the challenge for most developing country governments is to find the proper balance between centralized and decentralized arrangements and to link them in ways that promote development most effectively. The optimal mix is not easily determined. It shifts as social, economic, and political conditions change.

Given such complexity, a variety of criteria must be used to assess decentralization. We suggest the following:

1. The degree to which decentralization contributes to achieving broad political objectives, such as promoting political stability; mobilizing support and cooperation for national development policies; and providing heterogenous regions, interests, and communities with a stake in the survival of the political system.

2. The degree to which decentralization increases administrative effectiveness, by promoting greater coordination among units of the national government and between them and subnational administrative units, local governments, and nongovernmental organizations, or by encouraging closer cooperation among organizations to attain mutually acceptable development goals.

3. The degree to which decentralization contributes to promoting economic and managerial efficiency, by allowing governments at both the central and local levels to achieve development goals in a more cost-effective manner.

4. The degree to which decentralization increases government responsiveness to the needs and demands of various interest groups within society.

5. The degree to which decentralization contributes to greater self-determination and self-reliance among subordinate units of administration or nongovernment organizations in promoting development or meeting highly valued needs within society.

6. The <u>appropriateness</u> of the means by which policies and programs are designed and carried out to achieve the goals of decentralization, however they are defined.

For the reasons noted earlier, definitive conclusions about decentralization by any of these criteria are difficult to draw from recent experience. Although few in-depth and systematic evaluations have been made of the costs and benefit of recent efforts at decentralization, those assessments indicate that some of the standards of success have been met in some countries but not in others. Indeed, similar approaches to decentralization have produced opposite effects in different countries. In many Third World nations the stated objectives of decentralization have been achieved in some regions, provinces, or communities, but not in others. Some goals have been realized during initial stages of decentralization but not later. Nearly all developing countries have experienced serious administrative problems in implementing decentralization.

The Mixed Results of Decentralization Policies

Assessing decentralization at its face value--that is, by the degree to which power and responsibility for planning and managing development activities have actually been transferred from central government agencies to other organizations--would lead to pessimistic conclusions. For example, despite the attempts made in Kenya, Tanzania, and the Sudan during the 1970s to decentralize development planning and administration, their systems remain highly centralized today. The proliferation of public corporations, parastatal enterprises, special function authorities, and quasi-public institutes in Latin America has actually expanded the power and control of the national government at the expense of local governments (Harris 1983). Despite the apparent concern for decentralization in South and Southeast Asia, the results have often led to greater dependence of local administrative units on the center. Instances abound where innovative decentralization programs were centrally created but not linked to established local organizations and sources of political and financial support. As noted, authority is commonly delegated to local organizations, but they are not given the resources to perform their new functions. Local governments in most Asian countries, for example, still function as bureaucratic instruments of the center rather than as generators of alternative values, preferences, and aspirations. Local organizations thus cannot easily nurture political or administrative development; they act merely to extend centrally established priorities and controls. Local leaders are seen by central government officials merely as communicators and solicitors of support for national policies, rather than as channels through which the conditions and needs of local communities are articulated and made known to central planners and policymakers, or as mobilizers of local resources for promoting development from the "bottom up" (Friedman 1983).

A review of experience with decentralization in developing countries reveals that each form has advantages and disadvantages and that different countries have had different results from their experiments with it. For example, despite the slowness with which it has come about, decentralization has increased the access of local communities to centrally controlled resources in Morocco. A Communal Supply Fund (Fonds d'Equipement Communal, or FEC) is administered by the Caisse de Depots et de Gestion, a lending agency supervised by the Ministries of Finance and Interior and the Central Bank of Morocco. It loaned over 90 million dirhams (DH) in 1979, and close to 200 million DH in 1980. The government of Morocco estimates that in the period

1981-85, the FEC will loan 2.45 billion DG (US$490 million) to the country's 846 communes. Morocco's economic situation worsened considerably in 1980 and 1981. Though the verifying data are not available, it is most unlikely that these optimistic appropriations and planned expenditures were--or will be--met. Nonetheless, even smaller increases than those projected demonstrate a significant commitment to decentralization (Nellis, 1983a).

In the past, the Communal Supply Fund was drawn on mainly by the richer, urban communes, which had staff capable of submitting fundable proposals to the Caisse, and which were generally more creditworthy. From 1976 through 1978, two comparatively well-developed and urbanized regions, the Central and North-West, contained communes that obtained 70 percent of all FEC loans. The government's response to this situation of inequity has been to raise by a factor of ten the appropriation to its Local Authorities Development Fund, created in 1976, which provides grants to cover the capital costs of communes. The Local Authorities Development Fund granted some 950 million DH in the period 1978-80, and quasi-official government sources indicated that a total of three billion DH will be made available through this fund in the years 1981-85. Data on the regional distribution of grants made by this fund in the years 1978-80 show that the two most favored regions, Central and North-West, were awarded 34.4 percent of all grants. Since these regions contain the two largest cities in the country, the percentage of grants received cannot be too far out of line with the percentage of population they contain. The less populated East and Center-South regions received comparatively small percentages, while the lightly populated South--containing the recently incorporated and still contested territory of the former Spanish Sahara--received a disproportionately large amount. Although there can be no claim that perfect regional equity has been attained, it is clear that the distribution is far less skewed than it is for the loans of the Communal Supply Fund. Here is an instance in which a decentralization effort has had a positive impact on equity (Nellis 1983b).

Moreover, the government has increased direct transfers from the Treasury to local governments--from 100 million DH in 1973 to 270 million DH in 1979. This action improves the creditworthiness of the less favored communes. Equally important, in the late 1970s the Ministry of the Interior launched a large dual effort: (a) to increase the number and competence of local-level civil servants serving the communes, and (b) to instruct the communal council presidents and executive committees on how to identify, draw up, and submit development project proposals to the various funding bodies. The effort is especially important, since it is estimated that as many as half of the communal council presidents are illiterate. On the reasonable assumption that many councils would tend to choose their more educated members as presidents, it seems likely that the level of illiteracy of the councillors as a whole is greater than 50 percent (Nellis 1983a).

Even if all the money earmarked in the 1981-85 *Plan* for communal projects were actually allocated and spent, and even if all the glowing words about communal involvement in defining and implementing these projects were realized, Morocco would still have to be classed in the very first stages of devolution. The communal councils may eventually raise their own resources through local taxes; they do not do so now. The local governments may eventually receive a development appropriation that they can spend without regard to central guidelines, or without the review of a central authority; they cannot do so now. Many in Morocco think that such local liberties are inconceivable, even in the very long run.

The present undertaking is a cautious first step in which the communal councils and their supporting staff are to learn the ways of budget and project preparation. It is a tutorial program. As the king explained in 1975, "It is, for the elected representatives, a school where one learns how to manage a budget, organize action and execute plans, a school which trains citizens conscious of the true priorities and sensitive to the needs of the population." These are only first steps toward a decentralized local government system. But that they should arise in Morocco--with all its historical justifications for centralization--and that they should involve such large sums of money and numbers of staff, make them most unusual and promising first steps (Nellis 1983a).

Studies of deconcentration in Algeria, Libya, and Tunisia come to similar conclusions: the performance and impact of decentralized administrative units have been positive in some cases, but have not always matched the goals of decentralization policies. Control over financial resources continues to be centralized; local and regional organizations continue to have severe shortages of qualified personnel, and they lack the capacity to carry out the responsibilities transferred to them (Nellis 1983a). Evaluations of deconcentration in Ghana point out that the long delay in setting up local governments "results from a lack of political commitment to the new structure." In Ghana, neither central nor regional bureaucrats have given decentralization full political support: "Those at the center evidently are reluctant to accept any diminution in their decisionmaking powers, while regional officials show signs of wanting to retain control over their own field officers" (Tordoff 1980, p. 387).

These problems--cautious implementation, staff shortages, the uncertainty of the benefits, and retention of central control over finances--

are seen in other countries as well. Ever since decentralization was instituted in Nigeria, the new local governments have been able to undertake a larger number of projects--such as building health and maternity centers, elementary schools, water systems, markets, roads, and bridges--and to purchase equipment and supplies needed to maintain them. A serious problem in making decentralization work in Nigeria, however, has been the untimely and inadequate release of allocated funds. Often the funds that are allocated to local governments are not all distributed. Constant delays in delivering those that are distributed force local governments to slow down construction or to cancel some projects entirely (Idode 1980).

In Asia, meanwhile, the Small Farmers' Development Agency (SFDA) made a noticeable impact on increasing the incomes of poor farmers in many districts of India during the 1970s. The SFDA provided services and inputs that were easily distributed to individual households. Studies of one district, Alway, shows that the program was instrumental in increasing the number of irrigation tubewells, pumping equipment, and cattle. But it was less successful in constructing physical infrastructure, providing technical assistance, or strengthening local institutions. The reason was that, in most fiscal years, SFDA was able to allocate less than half the funds provided to it because it lacked enough trained staff. SFDA also suffered from rapid staff turnover and the unwillingness of local officials to innovate or to deal with local problems creatively, and had difficulty in translating central government guidelines into relevant local development activities. Throughout its life, the project remained dependent on the central government for funds and direction (Mathur 1982).

Similarly, Thailand's Rural Employment Generation Program (REG) was found to be very successful in Lampang Province, but not as successful in many other provinces. In 1980 and 1981, the decentralized REG projects in Lampang employed about 50,000 man-days of labor, provided work for 4,000-5,000 people each year, and increased the income of 2,000-3,000 rural households. Moreover, the program helped train local officials to plan, design, and carry out projects that were chosen in open meetings of tambon councils. Previously, projects were selected by higher level government officials and carried out entirely by contractors, with little or no participation by villagers. The Rural Employment Generation Program set in motion a process through which tambon leaders, according to one evaluation (Noranitipadungkarn 1982, pp. 52-53), "are learning how to conceive useful projects, how to get things done, how to mobilize people, how to communicate with officials and businessmen." Perhaps most important of all, it concludes, is that local leaders learned "how to work democratically through the whole process of implementation."

Yet, even in the successful provinces, there were some tambon leaders who did not commit the time and energy needed to make the program successful, and who attempted to select projects without the participation of villagers. In tambons that chose larger scale, more complex projects, there was a shortage of skilled technicians needed to design and implement them.

Pakistan's Integrated Rural Development Program (IRDP) in Manawala markaz has been evaluated as highly successful and that in Harrappa markaz as better than average. The determining factor seems to be that, in both areas, the markaz councils were quite active. They actually formulated, promoted, and carried out local development projects, the number and value of which increased over the years. Provincial governments provided much of the financing for local projects, but in each markaz people made contributions. The projects generally seemed to benefit a large segment of the population.

Yet, even in these success stories, the markaz councils were more successful in getting national ministries and agencies to provide infrastructure and social services than they were in coordinating inputs for agricultural development. Indeed, throughout the Punjab, local representatives of national ministries lacked the capacity to coordinate their agencies' activities and received little encouragement from their headquarters to do so. The technical assistance that the central ministries were able to offer was often inappropriate for small-scale projects. Thus, much of the success of the program in these two areas was attributable to the project managers' extraordinary personal ability to get local leaders to work together on self-help projects for which guidelines were clear and funds were readily available, and which did not necessarily depend on cooperation from national departments (Khan 1982).

Other studies of deconcentration support these conclusions. Uphoff and Esman (1974) point out that central government field officers in Bangladesh have an important role in formulating annual and middle-range development plans, in providing ministry services at the thana level, and in mobilizing resources for local services such as flood control and irrigation works, disaster relief, and fertilizer distribution. In Egypt, the field staff of central ministries at the governorate level have primary responsibility for delivering all rural services, including agriculture, irrigation, education, health, social welfare, and other programs. Provincial administrators in Indonesia help develop subnational programs for agriculture, public works, and rural finance; formulate district development plans; play a major role in setting local tax rates; and provide irrigation and extension services. In Malaysia nearly all extension, irrigation, health, education, and land development activities and some credit processing and marketing functions are provided in rural areas through the staffs of central and state departments at the district level. Similar functions are performed by field officers of central ministries or by subnational units of the central administration in the Philippines, Sri Lanka, Thailand, and Turkey.

But even when central agencies are deconcentrated in structure, many have a limited capacity to deliver services efficiently throughout the country. They are usually least effective in meeting the needs of the rural poor. Even deconcentrated field agencies of central government ministries have limited reach in extending their services, limited capacity to sustain local activities over a long period of time, and limited ability to adapt their programs and services to local needs and circumstances. Where they have established programs, some have created new forms of dependency for local communities (Korten 1983). Nor have delegation and privatization always been effective. The case of PERTAMINA--Indonesia's public enterprise controlling petroleum and energy investment--is often cited as an example of the problems of delegating monopoly control of a lucrative sector of the economy to a nearly autonomous public corporation. One analyst notes that during its peak of power in the mid-1970s, PERTAMINA invested so heavily and diversified so widely that it came to dominate other ministries and agencies and amassed sufficient political power to set its own policies and directions. Its activities came to influence the direction of Indonesia's entire economy. Its "size, power and wealth rival the sovereignty of its putative shareholder, the state itself," Fabrikant (1975, p. 529) points out. He concluded from his study of PERTAMINA that "when left alone, a state enterprise tends to deviate from the state's interest in an opportunistic direction. This demonstrates a principal danger of state enterprises: as they become powerful, they tend to assume identities apart from, and pursue interests inconsistent with, those of their shareholder." Later, when PERTAMINA's directors so overextended the corporation's resources that it was in danger of bankruptcy, it posed a serious threat to Indonesia's economic stability.

Lamb (1982, p. 4) points out that "market surrogate" strategies—that is, using private organizations to make public agencies more competitive or responsive to clientele groups—often work better in reaching the rural poor than does reliance entirely on the public sector:

> The Indonesia family planning program has used traditional itinerant herb vendors, alongside the public agency, to take contraceptives to remote rural areas. In Argentina, allowing private sector involvement in road maintenance has not only improved maintenance standards and generated entrepreneurial activity, it has also prompted contractor-like competitive innovation in the way the public agency conducts its own maintenance operations in parallel with the private sector. This has also been the approach the Bangladesh Agricultural Development Corporation used in liberalizing domestic marketing arrangements for fertilizer supply so as to increase competition between private dealers, and to retrench its own costly and ineffective structure at the thana level. The claimed accomplishment within two years of the early Chittagong Division experiment included better farmer access to points of sale, and lower fertilizer prices than under the old system.

Studies of community self-help programs in Nigeria indicate that this form of privatization has been effective in bringing unused local resources into production, in employing local labor, in relieving pressures on over-extended government agencies, and in increasing the skills and self-confidence of those participating in projects. In Kwara State, for example, local self-help groups were able to raise N20 million for health, education and infrastructure projects, more than 90 percent of which came from local contributions and only about 8 percent from central or state governments (Kolawole 1982). In Bendel State, private and voluntary organizations raised more than N37 million for schools, hospitals, roads, bridges, water systems, community halls, markets, and rural industries; and the government provided only about 13 percent of the expenditures (Okafor 1982).

But the privatization of these activities also had a tendency to create greater inequities among communities and regions with different levels of organizational capacity. It allowed local elites to play a dominant role in the planning and management of many projects. It gave, sometimes, a disproportionate amount of influence to wealthier families, who proposed and carried out projects primarily benefiting themselves. Indeed, one study indicated that this form of privatization allowed influential elites and families to put pressure on poor families to contribute to projects from which they received little or no benefits (Kalawole 1983).

Devolution, where it has been tried seriously, also has produced mixed results. On the positive side, evaluations of devolution in Papua New Guinea point out that the "introduction of provincial government has increased participation in government and provided a much greater opportunity for people to participate in decisionmaking in their own areas" (Conyers 1981, p. 223). Early indications are that the creation of provincial governments has improved the planning, management, and coordination capacity of provincial administrators. It has contributed strongly to attracting skilled technicians and professionals to return to work in their own provinces. Devolution has been less successful, however, in ameliorating provincial inequalities and disparities in levels of development (Hinchliffe 1980; Berry and Jackson 1981). Moreover, the World Bank's economic mission to Papua New Guinea reports that devolution has had a mixed impact on the country's economy. Although it seems to have made the government more responsive to local needs, "decentralization has opened up a new set of problems," the mission (1982, pp. 9-10) reports. "It has weakened the control of the central government over planning and implementation of its expenditures." The mission found that central government grants to provincial governments have allowed them to create new public services that have very high per capita administrative costs and for the maintenance of which the provinces lack local sources of revenue. Moreover, the addition of another layer of bureaucracy with which potential investors must deal further weakens the central government's capacity to stimulate economic growth. The lessening of central control over expenditure has had the effect, at least in the initial stages of decentralization, of increasing rather than ameliorating provincial inequalities in public and social services (Hinchliffe 1980).

Provinces in Papua New Guinea are almost totally dependent on the central government for their revenues. Revenues from the provinces accounted for less than 6 percent of all provincial expenditures in 1978, and in 1981 rose to less than 8.5 percent. The amount of unconditional grants to the provinces increased by 65 percent between 1978 and 1981. Other forms of central revenues increased by 45 percent over the four fiscal years. Transfers to provinces accounted for 20-25 percent of all central government outlays (see Table 1).

Decentralization as an Incremental Process of Capacity Building

The studies of decentralizaton reviewed here reveal a kind of schizophrenia in developing countries about the desirability and feasibility of transferring powers and responsibilities away from the central government. That is, local administrative units have, in theory, been given broad powers to perform development planning and management functions; but adequate financial resources and qualified personnel to carry them out have been withheld. In some countries, devolution has involved a transfer, from

Table 1 Provincial Government Revenues in Papua New Guinea, 1978-81
(K'000)

Type of Revenue	1978	1979	1980	1981 a/
Unconditional Grants				
Provincial minimum grants	20,216	38,579	45,946	49,446
Office of Implementation b/	51,359	64,446	67,448	75,331
Provincial salaries c/	3,007	8,031	14,215	...
Subtotal	75,582	111,056	127,609	124,777
Provincially Based Revenue				
Provincial derivation grants	421	3,377	2,191	2,849
Betting tax/license grant	96	101	277	230
Liquor licenses	553	...	...	...
Tobacco and cigarette sales tax	...	...	1,109	1,250
Mining royalties	1,904	3,827	4,026	3,875
Timber royalties	1,046	1,423	1,415	1,680
Motor registration and licenses	701	1,128	136	2,800
Subtotal	4,721	9,856	9,154	12,684
Establishment grants d/	422	...	...	...
Operational grants	97	...	...	...
Provincial development corporations	490	1,973	...	...
Staffing grants	...	685	877	943
Provincial capital works	98	1,454	...	340
Provincial maintenance (roads)	...	...	1,589	1,600
National Fiscal Commission	1,365	5,000	7,000	5,000
National Public Expenditure Plan Projects e/	5,394	1,963	1,372	334
Simbu works and maintenance	...	...	...	2,763
Kerema Kantiba road	...	...	...	400
Subtotal	7,866	11,075	10,838	11,380
Total	88,169	132,088	147,601	148,841

a/ Budget estimate.
b/ Branch of Department of Decentralization responsible for provinces which do not have full financial autonomy. Includes 15 provinces in 1980, 16 in 1979, and 18 in 1978.
c/ Includes 1 province in 1978; 3 in 1979; 4 in 1980 and 1981.
d/ A one-time grant for each province.
e/ Excludes sectoral programs. They are included in the central government budget.

Source: World Bank, Papua New Guinea: Selected Development Issues (Washington, D.C. 1982), p. 87.

the central to the subnational level or levels, of the capacity to tax or otherwise raise revenues. In most cases these powers have been severely circumscribed and limited. Personal property and real estate taxes, cesses on sellers and buyers in local markets, school fees, portions of income derived from locally marketed natural resources (for example, forest products), and profits derived from industries owned and operated by local authorities are but a few of the ways in which local governments have been able, when so empowered, to self-generate revenues. In most developing countries, both the revenue-raising powers transferred and the sums so far raised have been very modest. But autonomous financial responsibility is at the core of the concept of decentralization. If the movement is to be serious, then it must involve large increases, first, in the power of subnational units to raise revenues, and, second, in the sums that are actually generated. These are not at all the same thing; in many countries decentralized units possess the legal authority to impose taxes, but the tax base is so weak and the dependency on central subsidies so ingrained that no attempt is made to implement the theoretical power. There is some evidence to support the view that substantial amounts of local resources lie untapped in even quite poor countries. The <u>Harambee</u> self-help movement in Kenya demonstrated that large sums could be raised from poor rural people if projects are aimed at clearly felt needs. Still, one does not easily see government officers raising revenues through these principles. The point is that, although many observers see the need for generating vastly increased local revenues (through taxation, charges, user fees, and sales), the prospects for this seem rather long-term.

That being so clearly the case, those involved in decentralization have a fallen back on the simpler process of transferring not power but resources to subnational levels. Some of the more common arrangements are:

portions of national taxes, or the whole of certain nationally imposed and collected taxes, are specified for the exclusive use of local governments; the central Ministry of the Interior directly subsidizes the recurrent or capital (or both) budgets of the subnational units; central ministries provide grants for local infrastructure development; banks or quasi-bank authorities provide loans and grants for capital projects; and funds derived from international assistance agencies are channeled toward subnational units of greatest need or potential. This transfer of resources, rather than the real power to self-generate resources, is very much the norm. It is less threatening to the central authorities. It reduces the burden, but increases the dependency, of local authorities, who generally neither impose taxes nor have to justify to local populations how revenues have been spent. It fits in neatly with the still prevailing ethos of planned, government-led economic organization. At worst, it is a means of cynically claiming to decentralize while retaining the crucial financial power in central hands. But at best, it can be seen as a reasonable response to the question of how one turns over to poverty-stricken and personnel-short local authorities the responsibility for complex development activities. As discussed later in the paper, a frequent answer is: start small, proceed incrementally, and vest financial control in central supervisors.

Field offices of central ministries, provincial planning and administrative units, and district and local development committees have been established in most countries in Asia and Africa, yet central government officials have been reluctant to assist them, or use them in other than a "transmission belt" manner. Local officials have been hesitant to use their discretion, and local officials continue to look to central government ministries for decisions even in routine matters. In their desire to minimize

political conflicts, governments in Third World countries have discouraged
potentially troublesome community and nongovernment organizations that appear
well placed to support and carry out decentralization policies. Thus, even
when opportunities are created for greater involvement in decisionmaking by
local groups, the intended beneficiaries often lack the organizational
capacities to take advantage of them (Cheema 1938).

But if decentralization is viewed as an <u>incremental process</u> of
building the capacity of subordinate or semiautonomous organizations to assume
greater responsibility for development planning and management, the slow,
halting, and hesitant pace of decentralization should be expected. Despite
the apparent schizophrenia of central government leaders and the pervasive
technical and administrative problems involved in transferring
responsibilities, there have been some positive results of the
decentralization policies that were enacted during the 1970s and early
1980s. From this perspective, the record of decentralization has been mixed,
but the problems are identifiable and potentially solvable.

Among the positive results of decentralization are the following.
First, the access of people living in previously neglected rural regions and
local communities to central government resources and institutions has
increased, if only incrementally, in most developing countries that have
decentralized. Second, decentralization seems in some places to have
increased participation. It has enlarged the capacity of local administrative
and political leaders to put pressure on central government agencies. Larger
amounts of national resources for local development have been made
available. Third, there are countries in which the administrative and
technical capability of regional and local organizations is slowly improving,
although usually not fast enough to perform all of the functions formally

assigned to them. Fourth, new organizations have been established at the regional and local levels to plan and manage development. These include regional development agencies, departmental development corporations, parastatal institutions, and semiautonomous organizations in Latin America and Africa. In Asia, provincial development planning committees have been created in Thailand, state planning units in Malaysia, regional development councils in the Philippines, provincial development planning boards in Indonesia, and special purpose development organizations in Pakistan and India. All of these have had a modestly positive impact. Finally, regional and local level planning is now being increasingly emphasized as an important component of national development strategy, bringing new perspectives and interests into the decisionmaking process (Rondinelli 1983).

Thus, although evaluations of decentralization show a mixed record of success, governments are moving cautiously but perceptibly toward greater deconcentration or delegation of development management. Although the data do not allow one to evaluate the impacts of decentralization definitively or to assess the economic costs and benefits of decentralized management procedures, the conditions that have affected the implementation of decentralization programs can be identified and discussed with some confidence.

V. Conditions and Factors Affecting the Implementation of Decentralization

In general, assessments of decentralization in developing countries suggest that four main factors affect the success or failure of these policies: (1) the degree to which central political leaders and bureaucracies support decentralization and the organizations to which responsibilities are transferred; (2) the degree to which the dominant behavior, attitudes, and culture are conducive to decentralized decisionmaking and administration; (3) the degree to which policies and programs are appropriately designed and organized to promote decentralized decisionmaking and management; and (4) the degree to which adequate financial, human, and physical resources are made available to the organizations to which responsibilities are transferred.

Degree of Political Commitment and Administrative Support

The degree to which national political leaders are committed to decentralizing planning and administrative functions, the ability and willingness of the national bureaucracy to facilitate and support decentralized development activities, and the capacity of field officials of national agencies and departments to coordinate their activities at the local level, all strongly influence the success of decentralized management.

The limited impact of decentralization in East Africa can be attributed largely to the weak political commitment of most national leaders and of many field officials and local leaders. In both Tanzania and the Sudan, decentralization and participation were promulgated by strong-willed presidents, who often received weak support from the bureaucracy and from their own political parties. Advocates of decentralization had to exert a good deal of pressure to convince other political leaders of the merits of bottom-up planning and decisionmaking. In the Sudan, the president had to reiterate these themes almost constantly for a decade. Even then, support for devolution remained shallow. Some central government officials believed that devolution would fragment the country and allow regional leaders to build semiautonomous fiefdoms. Others argued that shifting functions to the provinces would weaken the central government's control over development and would maintain the provincialism that had prevented the Sudan from achieving national unity. In Kenya, decentralization was advocated primarily by expatriate advisers and a small group of leaders in the central government, with some support by tribal or regional leaders who saw it as a way of strengthening their positions in the competition for resources. There is little evidence to suggest that widespread political support existed for decentralized decisionmaking. In all three countries, strong leadership was required over a long period of time to make even limited forms of decentralization politically palatable (Rondinelli 1981a).

In Kenya and the Sudan, national bureaucracies supported decentralization policies only reluctantly. In Tanzania, the bureaucracy backed decentralization and villagization policies only halfheartedly, even after coming under the control of the dominant political party. National ministry officials in the Sudan resented the transfer of their functions to the provinces. Only the complete abolition of some ministries removed the most intransigent bureaucratic obstacles--at least temporarily--and served notice to other ministries that their cooperation was mandatory. Less drastic measures in Tanzania and Kenya left the central ministries in control of lower levels of administration or allowed them to reconsolidate power and authority within regional or provincial administrations.

In North Africa, there has been opposition to decentralization within the national bureaucracies. It has been rationalized by the argument that in time of war or national emergency most industrialized countries have relied on governments with strong centralized powers and controls. Therefore, Third World countries, which are plagued by ethnic divisions, dismal economic performance, and myriad other system-threatening conditions, must take firm steps to impose a modicum of national integrity on their weak and fragile polities. Underdevelopment is the poor countries' "moral equivalent of war." The enemies--poverty, ignorance, and disease--are so apparent and so pervasive, that a quasi-military, heirarchical, centralized form of organization is considered to be not only defensible, but absolutely necessary. In Morocco, opposition to decentralization has been officially recognized and castigated (Royaume de Maroc 1981, p. 73):

> Certain obstacles linked to the implementation of new decentralized institutions continue to hinder the application of options taken by the Government. These difficulties concern the reticence of a certain number of central services to cede prerogatives—implementation, launching of actions, recruitment and management of personnel—to their field units judged still too inexperienced and insufficiently endowed in human and physical terms. The functions of these services must be redefined in order to permit them to play fully the role which is assigned to them in the processes of decentralization and deconcentration.

The weakness of political support for decentralization in many Asian countries is illustrated by studies of voluntary organizations. Despite the proliferation of voluntary groups in the region, their overall impact on rural development has been, and continues to be, minimal. Most governments are simply not willing to tolerate the politicization and potential conflict that independent, nongovernment, organizations can create in rural areas. Thus, only those that have been established by the government or that assist central agencies in implementing their programs are likely to survive and grow (Cheema 1983).

As in Morocco, decentralization has been undermined in some Asian countries because the national civil service opposed arrangements that threatened its power and control. In the 1970s in Sri Lanka, for example, civil service unions protected the prerogatives of central administrators during attempts to decentralize development planning and management. They intervened actively in the political process to prevent a diffusion of administrative responsibility. Wanasinghe (1982, pp. 49-50) points out that,

> The general thrust of these interventions has been toward maintaining individuality and autonomy of respective departmental cadres, strengthening the role of the bureaucracy in decisionmaking, enhancing career prospects through island-wide services. These thrusts have continuously run counter to attempts at implementation of local area-focussed coordination, delegated decision-making by peoples' respresentatives, and creation of self-management organizations with their own personnel.

As a result, even when strong pressures came from the prime minister to coordinate activities within districts, many field officers resisted: "The technical department cadres continued to maintain their allegiance to their own departments rather than to the district organization." Field officers considered the district a temporary assignment. Their commitment was to national headquarters, where decisions about their promotion, salaries, and assignments continued to be made.

Even in areas where Pakistan's IRDP was successful, the support and cooperation of the national departments remained weak. Evaluations of the program in Mananwala and Harappa found that representatives of some national agencies rarely attended meetings of the markaz council. The project manager could get little support on technical matters from some national departments. Often, the kinds of advice they provided were inappropriate for small-scale local development projects. In neither markaz did representatives of most national departments receive adequate financial resources or transportation from their headquarters to be able to attend frequent coordinating meetings or to supervise their activities in the field. The IRDP approach did not fit well with the operating procedures of most national agencies, and they made little effort to change their ways of doing things (Khan 1982).

On the other hand, strong political and administrative support for decentralization in other Asian countries did have a profoundly positive influence on development programs. The Rural Employment Generation Program in

Thailand, for example, attained many of its goals precisely because it had the special attention of the prime minister, who chaired its national committee. This committee included heads of the national ministries and departments whose support was needed to push the program at the province and tambon levels. The strong interest of the prime minister assured that the program had high priority among cabinet ministers.

Central political support was crucial in initiating district level coordination of agricultural programs in Sri Lanka in the late 1960s. But district coordination was only successful as long as the prime minister gave it personal attention and handpicked senior administrators to serve as government agents. When the prime minister's attention turned to other matters, senior administrators returned to the capital and were not replaced by people of equal status. The "monitoring visits" of high-level officials then became less frequent. The ability of government agents to coordinate the activities of national departments within the districts waned quickly.

Wherever the IRDP was successful in Pakistan, it was partly because of the attention it received from high-level political leaders and officials. "Frequent visits by the national elites and the representatives of donor agencies created necessary compulsions for the national departments to demonstrate their commitment to the project by opening up their offices at or near the markaz complex," Khan (1982, p. 67) notes. Furthermore, "as the Project Manager got better access to his senior colleagues, logistical support to this markaz also improved." These factors helped the successful markaz to attract more resources and physical infrastructure and thus stay in the lead.

Attitudinal, Behavioral, and Cultural Conditions Conducive to Decentralization

Effectiveness in implementing decentralized programs appears to depend largely on the presence of appropriate behavioral, attitudinal, and cultural conditions. The most important factors include: the willingness of local officals to support and perform decentralized management functions, the quality of local leadership, the attitudes of rural people toward government, and the degree to which traditional customs and behavior are compatible with decentralized procedures for planning, decisionmaking, and management. All of these are "soft" variables; they are difficult to deal with in a policy or operational sense. Yet, clearly, they are important.

The attitudes and behavior of central and local government officials toward the citizenry are crucial (perhaps especially so in countries with long histories of colonization) in determining whether or not decentralization will be effective.

Studies of administrative behavior in North Africa note that the excessively centralized planning and implementation systems are a reflection of the patronizing, rigid manner in which superiors direct their subordinates on what to do and how to do it, and the equally lofty manner in which these subordinates pass on these instructions, eventually, to the citizenry at large (Apthorpe 1977). This syndrome cannot be blamed entirely on the colonial tradition, for many of these countries have had more than twenty-five years to divest themselves of unwanted patterns. Algeria, for example, has had both the resources and the opportunities to bring about drastic change during its twenty-one years of independence. Certainly, much of the reinforcement of the inherited centralist system can be explained by internal causes. Nonetheless, the basic framework for a paternalistic, condescending, authoritarian, and highly centralized system was created by colonialists. In short, in North Africa the colonial rulers instituted, or at least reinforced, the belief that the citizen exists to serve the state, and not the reverse. Colonial governance in general and colonial bureaucracy in particular were neatly, strictly hierarchical. The function of subsidiary units was to obey the center's directives; the function of the center was to direct. A centralist philosophy was strongly supported by administrative procedures and accounting systems that vested all authority and monitoring functions in the center. The aphorism was easily applied to all four capitals. "Everything starts in (Paris, Rabat, Algiers, Tunis); everything finishes in (Paris, Rabat, Algiers, Tunis)." This set of attitudes persists (Nellis 1983a).

The attitudes and behavior of central government officials have also obstructed decentralization in Latin America. Harris (1983), noting the lack of trust central administrators have in officials from the regions, concluded that:

> It is difficult to determine whether this is a product of what has been referred to as the centrist mentality of national officials or is a well founded concern over the shortage of highly skilled and trained officials in the regions. But the result is a wide-spread reluctance on the part of central government officials to delegate power to regional and sub-regional levels. This has resulted in a "yo-yo" process of delegation and withdrawal of delegation, depending upon whether the central officials are satisfied or not with the decisions and actions taken by officials in the region.

In a number of Asian countries--India, Pakistan, Sri Lanka, and Malaysia--national government officials proved unwilling to give local administrators discretion in carrying out local development functions, this demonstrating their centrist bias. In Malaysia, state and district officers of the Federal Agricultural Marketing Authority (FAMA)--are given virtually no autonomy in making decisions, even though they deal with unique and quickly changing conditions. They lack control, or even influence, over the prices they pay for crops or the disposition of the products they acquire. This severely constrains their ability to react flexibly in carrying out the authority's mandate. The assistant state FAMA officers work at the district level in daily interaction with the farmers. They can only make recommendations to FAMA headquarters in Kuala Lumpur, where all operating decisions are made. Thus, "although he is, to all intents and purposes, the chief businessman for the Agricultural Marketing Center," Nor Ghani (1982 p. 16) points out, "he cannot conduct business according to his own terms and must continuously be guided by FAMA headquarters in Kuala Lumpur."

The success of Indonesia's Provincial Development Program (PDP) in Madura, on the other hand, has been attributed in large part to the strong support it has received from provincial and local officials. Most proved willing or have been persuaded to take on the additional work entailed in making decentralization effective. PDP, and especially the small village credit program that is a part of it, is labor intensive. The official's time must be allocated to a large number of new and unfamiliar tasks, including initiating "bottom-up" planning, selecting target group participants, setting up new administrative arrangements that are responsive to local conditions and needs, training local leaders to manage the programs, implementing the projects, monitoring and evaluating their progress, and preparing requests for reimbursements (Moeljarto 1982).

In areas where the small-scale credit schemes work best, one evaluation found, "the village head plays more than a _pro forma_ role and does the groundwork for the operation of the program." Leaders explain to the villagers the objectives of the program and their rights and obligations. After these preparations have been made, village leaders, the officials of the small village credit program, and other community leaders--with some guidance from the subdistrict head--select those to receive loans. This process is open, participatory, and cooperative, and these factors presumably account for the smooth operation of the program and the good record of loan repayments in successful villages. "The result is remarkable," Moeljarto (1982) observed. "The commitments of all local leaders as minifested in their cooperative behavior and shared responsibility becomes one of the keys to the success of the program..." In villages where this leadership and cooperation were lacking, loans were often based on favoritism and were often made to high-risk borrowers. The result was many bad debts.

The success of the small village credit program in many communities in Madura is also due to the ability of officials to obtain the cooperation of influential informal leaders and to overcome the potentially adverse effects of traditional behavior. Officials took great pains, for example, to accommodate the beliefs of local religious leaders who subscribed to the Koranic injunction against paying interest. These officials and the orthodox Kyais, who served not only as religious but also as informal community leaders, agreed to use the term "management fee" instead of interest. Throughout the program, officials and Kyais maintained close communication and cooperated in setting up and operating the credit organizations.

Implementation of decentralization in East Africa, however, was hampered by the rural population's distrust of government officials and their unwillingness to believe the government's promises. This mutual distrust often led local staff to identify and select projects without consulting rural people. That behavior encouraged local residents to sabotage, undermine, or simply ignore development projects that they did not want or understand, or that they felt were not in their interests. Rural people refused to participate in family planning clinics in some areas of Kenya because they misunderstood their intent. They did not allow land to be used for agricultural demonstrations in other places, fearing that the government would later take over the improved property. Rural road construction was disrupted by some rural villagers who thought that the new roads would allow government patrols to catch stock raiders more easily (Mbithi and Barnes 1975). Because they did not always understand the rationale for programs chosen by regional or district officials, villagers in Tanzania often refused to participate in local development activities and limited their involvement to projects providing immediate social benefits--such as schools, clinics, and water supply facilities--for which the central government paid recurrent costs.

The persistent influence and sometimes dominance of local elites in most African countries are partly explained by the widespread acceptance of paternalistic leadership. In much of East Africa the interaction between traditional leaders and peasants is hierarchical. Leaders protect their authority by discouraging others from making decisions without their consent or consultation. Thus, rural people are often reluctant to challenge local elites who oppose decentralization, and subordinate officials are hesitant to take action that would upset their superiors. The strong dependence of rural people on traditional leaders is difficult to break simply by creating new organizations or planning procedures (Nellis 1973; El Bashir 1976; Moris 1976).

All of this implies that if decentralization is to be effective, the attitudes and behavior of both central government officials and local leaders must be altered to recognize the value and legitimacy of shared decisionmaking and more widespread participation in development planning and management. Control-oriented and paternalistic attitudes are incompatible with the philosophy of decentralization. Training programs must emphasize the facilitative roles that the civil service can perform in a decentralized system. Attention must be given to overcoming the resistance--and attaining the cooperation--of local elites and traditional leaders. Ultimately, the successful implementation of decentralization requires trust and respect between citizens and public officials, and recognition of the important roles that each can perform in the development process. In planning decentralization programs, therefore, provisions must be made for strengthening leadership and administrative capacity within rural communities, and for mobilizing the leadership, knowledge, and skills that already exists.

Effective Design and Organization of Decentralization Programs

Organization variables influence the outcomes of decentralization efforts. They include the clarity and simplicity of the structures and procedures used to decentralize, the ability of the implementing agency staff to interact with higher level authorities, and the degree to which components of decentralized programs are integrated.

Uncertainty about exactly how to implement decentralization was pervasive in both the Sudan and Tanzania. Province executive councils in the Sudan received little technical assistance from the center and the Tanzania government issued few guidelines on implementing the ujamaa village policy. In the absence of guidance or technical assistance, many decisions were made arbitrarily. Essential services were not provided in many ujamaa villages before families were moved in, and sites for the villages were often chosen to benefit richer farmers and traders rather than the peasants (Kjekshus 1977; von Freyhold 1976; Hyden 1976; Ergas 1980).

In Asian countries where decentralization programs were organized in a way that made their purposes and procedures uncomplicated, these programs were more successful than in countries where the purposes were ambiguous and the procedures were complex. For example, the goals of the SFDA in India were overly ambitious and its procedures were difficult to apply locally. There was a large gap between the rhetoric of central planners and what they were willing to allow local administrators to do. Mathur (1982 p. 69) contends that "At the central level the planners usually talked in high ideal tones and insisted that the local level officials needed to respond to local situations and not to central instructions." They told local officials that the most important goal of the program was to raise the income of beneficiaries and that loans and subsidies were only a means to that end and not ends in themselves. But "these ideas somehow failed to percolate down." In reality, SFDA staff were shackled by detailed central rules and regulations, many of which were inapplicable at the local level. Evaluations were based on the number of loans made rather than their impact on beneficiaries. The banks that made the loans to small-scale farmers were, perhaps inevitably, more concerned with repayment than with the effects on agricultural production.

Moreover, the multiple levels of review and approval through which local plans have had to pass in many countries, created delays that discouraged enthusiastic participation in decentralized planning and management. Complexity of procedures, so it seems, consistently reinforces the power of the bureaucracy to veto or modify proposals and creates greater uncertainty and perplexity among the citizenry.

This is not an argument for doing away with regulations, though certainly many advocates of privatization and debureaucratization could interpret it as such. The more modest point here is that procedures should be based on the principles of simplicity and clarity. In Indonesia and Thailand, clearly defined purposes and procedures allowed programs to progress more smoothly and effectively in many areas. Noranitipadungkarn (1982, p. 60) points out that "the central government has carefully laid down the responsibility and the authority, as well as the expected roles of respective levels of government." In Indonesia, rules and procedures were realistic and designed to be applicable at the local level. Province officials guided and supervised the program to ensure that it was carried out effectively, but left room for local initiative and flexibility. Frequent visits by provincial planning agency and sectoral staff from Surabaya to Madura were made to guide, supervise, and monitor local activities. This behavior not only motivated local officials but created a system of checks and balances that improved implementation (Moeljarto 1982).

Another factor severely inhibiting the successful implementation of decentralization policies has been the inability of local agencies to coordinate and integrate their activities with those of central ministries. Centralization here both causes and reinforces ineffective coordination. Proliferation of government agencies has led to compartmentalization and lack of complementarity, which have further weakened the administrative capacities of local agencies.

The difficulty of coordinating development activities in some Asian countries has been due in part to the low status of the officials placed in charge of decentralized programs. The staff of the Small Farmers Development Agency in India, for example, did not have fixed tenure, and their behavior was influenced by the knowledge that they would be transferred frequently (Mathur 1982).

In Pakistan, IRDP project managers had virtually no formal powers to compel cooperation by representatives of national departments. Whatever success they achieved at the markaz level depended on their individual skills in persuading field officers and heads of local organizations to participate in council activities. They had no formal organizational structure that facilitated integration of national efforts at the local level.

Overall, the disappointing results of decentralization in Africa and Asia can be explained, first, by the absence of, or weaknesses in, supporting institutions--both public and private--needed to complement and bolster the managerial capacity of local governments, and, second, by the weaknesses in linkages and interaction between central and local administrations. Experiences with decentralization in different parts of the Third World have demonstrated that a wide variety of institutions must contribute to local development, and that they must be complementary and integrated. Services and technologies supporting local development must mutually reinforce each other in a systematic way. Credit delivered without technical assistance, without higher yielding seed varieties, without fertilizers and irrigation, and without improved marketing, for instance, has little impact on agricultural production in rural areas. Institutions must be linked both vertically and horizontally to provide a hierarchy of services and to increase the quality and reliability of service delivery. In their studies of local organization in Asia, Uphoff and Esman (1974 pp. xi-xii) "found no case where only one institution was carrying the full responsibility for rural development and where complementarities among institutions were not as important as what the institutions themselves did."

David Leonard (1977, p. 10) also concluded from his study of the organization of agricultural development in Kenya that "the key concept in rural administration is linkages. The days of autonomous agricultural development are ended. The development of the small farm sector is critically dependent on government support. The state develops new agricultural technologies, promotes and finances their acceptance and determines the dynamism of their growth through price and other controls." At the same time, central government alone cannot stimulate and sustain local development.

Ultimately, progress depends on the initiative of individual leaders and organizations in conjunction with the support they receive from higher level authorities.

The importance of linkages between central and local organizations is emphasized in nearly all studies of decentralization. Analysts of decentralization in Africa have found that supporting linkages must be created between central and local governments in order to overcome weaknesses in administrative capacity at lower levels of government. Such linkages are likely to produce more positive local responses to national development priorities than central regulations and controls. There are several ways in which central government agencies can provide assistance to weak local administrations: by offering training; by seconding personnel from central agencies to meet pressing staff shortages at the local level; by supervising and assessing local projects and providing technical assistance when problems or weaknesses appear; and by creating a national cadre to supply personnel to agencies at provincial, district, and local levels (Leonard 1983). Morocco is one of the few countries doing all of these things.

Leonard (1983) also notes some of the limitations of creating assistance linkages: the conditions necessary for supporting local agencies may not exist, as was the case in Tanzania; some assistance linkages may ultimately become control mechanisms, thereby increasing local dependence. And once the linkages are forged, they may be used as instruments by national agencies to further extend their influence in rural areas. Rather than creating a more effective partnership between national and local governments, linkages could be used to increase the penetration of central authority into the countryside.

What can be done to promote more effective cooperation between central and local organizations? In most North African states, where problems of coordination and cooperation have been very serious, a fundamental first step would be to change the traditional process of supervision, especially fiscal supervision, by central authorities of the actions of local or subordinate units. This practice--<u>tutelle</u>--was a keystone of the inherited system, and it has been polished and buttressed ever since independence. The concept is deeply embedded in the Maghrebian legal and administrative framework; and thus it is unthinkable that it could be eliminated totally. But it is conceivable that the supervision system could be relaxed or abolished, on a trial basis, for a limited range of actions--of the type such as the PDR in Tunisia, for example (see Annex 3). The added responsibilities might stimulate local endeavor. Competent local performance, in turn, might persuade national officials of the feasibility of further relaxation. Of course, it is possible that local officials, freed from higher level review, might channel resources toward goals that conflict with national priorities. Worse, local authorities might manage programs so poorly as to call into question the entire venture. Precisely because of these risks, one must start small, with limited arenas of action. These efforts must be treated as an experiment. Ideally, they would be supported by additions of trained staff; but everywhere this is the scarcest of resources.

Studies of decentralization in Africa and Asia suggest that the functions transferred to local administrative units must be suited to their current or potential managerial capacities. Functions should be allocated to local units incrementally, as they meet performance criteria. More complex functions should be transferred only after local units increase their administrative capacities and resources. Decentralization laws must be written concisely and regulations should describe clearly and simply the relationships and obligations of officials and citizens, the allocation of functions among units, and the roles and duties of leaders at each level. The procedures for local participation in development management must be kept relatively simple and should not require special technical skills or resources that would exclude all but the elite. They should be kept flexible. Communications systems should facilitate mutual interaction, exchange of information, cooperation, and conflict resolution, rather than simply disseminating instructions from the central government and gathering information from below. To be sure, it is much easier to list what is needed than it is to state exactly how to bring about the needed changes.

Adequate Financial, Human, and Physical Resources

One of the dilemmas of decentralization is that it is central government officials who take the initiative, usually under pressure from other groups, to decentralize authority. They then, all too often, negate that authority by refusing to transfer financial, administrative, and technical resources to local agencies. Studies of decentralization in Kenya, the Sudan, and Tanzania show the crucial efffects of shortages of trained manpower on the success of decentralization in those countries. National ministries, public corporations, and other central government agencies attracted the most skilled technicians and the best educated managers, leaving a chronic shortage of talent at the local level. Leadership and management training courses for local officials were not adequate (Rondinelli 1982).

In Kenya the vast majority of skilled technicians and managers were concentrated in Nairobi. But as USAID evaluators (1979b, p. 5) have pointed out, "the numbers of adequately trained personnel are sufficient to meet only the principal needs for the top levels of the public and private sectors."

Even top-level administrators had only minimal technical training and little or no managerial experience. The analysts concluded that "management capability at this and the middle level is woefully lacking and is having an increasingly negative impact on implementation of development programs." The Sudan had the most severe shortages of skilled personnel, even within central ministries. Devolution, and the brain drain of technically skilled Sudanese to high-paying jobs in Saudi Arabia and other oil-exporting countries, added to the problem. Personnel shortages seriously impeded decentralization in the Sudan and limited the ability of provincial administrators to provide even basic services (Rondinelli 1981b).

Morocco is one of the few countries in Africa that has recognized the importance of providing adequate personnel at the local level to carry out decentralized planning and management. To assist the elected local councils in their expanded tasks, the central government in 1977 created a special new corps of posts in the local civil service. By 1980 each of the 85 urban and semiurban communes had received a new official, a centrally trained and paid chief civil servant called the secretary-general. All rural communes will eventually receive secretaries-general; the first contingent of about 90 graduated from a special six-month training course in mid-1982. It will probably be four or five years before all 761 rural communes have a secretary-general in post. These officials are vital, since it will largely be their ability to formulate projects in an acceptable manner that will allow the rural communes to tap the expanded centrally controlled investment funds.

The expansion of establishments and training for local civil servants is another indicator of Moroccan commitment to decentralization. In 1979 the number of civil servants serving subnational units was increased by 20 percent over 1977 levels. Between 1968 and 1980, Ministry of Interior training centers graduated a total of 2,309 people. In 1981 alone, a rapidly expanded complement of thirteen training centers, under the active supervision of a new Training Division of the Ministry of the Interior, had an enrollment of 2,334 students--a larger number than had received training in the previous twelve years (Nellis 1983a).

The shortages of skilled staff at the local level has been an equally important factor in the implementation of decentralization in Asia. Many programs are plagued with a chronic lack of trained technicians and managers. SFDA in India was especially weakened by the rapid turnover of personnel within districts. An evaluation of the programs in Alway District, for example, found that the average tenure of the district collector, who headed SFDA, had been 17 months, and of the project officer, 18 months. In one rare instance, a project officer stayed for 48 months, but during his term there were three changes in district collector, two in agricultural project officer, two in the animal husbandry officer, and five in the cooperatives officer. The knowledge that posts were temporary gave local officers little incentive to take responsibility or to build effective teams to coordinate their activities (Mathur 1982). Similarly, in Sri Lanka the officers assigned to the districts saw them as temporary appointments and were not willing to take risks that would threaten their promotion or reassignment. In Pakistan, the technical personnel available to the markaz councils have been quite limited--sometimes only one engineer is available to assist with projects in the fifty to sixty villages within the markaz. Moreover, project managers are often not trained to do their jobs; most are either agricultural technicians or generalist administrators who have little or no experience with areawide planning and development (Khan 1982).

Inadequate technical and managerial skills also limit the political influence of local agencies in most developing countries. Citizens continue to look to the center rather than to local organizations for resources and approval for their projects. Under these conditions, the morale of local administrators remains low and their skills remain weak. Eventually many lose what commitment they may have had to local development.

The inadequacy of financial resources and the inability to allocate and expand them effectively were noted in evaluations of decentralization in nearly every developing country. The lack of independent sources of revenue weakened the SFDA's ability to carry out its tasks in India. The dependence on central government grants kept the SFDA under the control of the central bureaucracy. Even in countries such as Fiji, which devolved revenue raising powers to local governments, localities remain dependent on central funding for most of their activities. After more than a decade of devolution in Fiji, the provincial councils still receive about 55 percent of their revenues from central government grants (Ali and Gunasekera 1982). In Morocco, the central government continues to support 65 percent of the expenditures of local authorities.

Limited financial resources and the shortages of investment capital in the Sudan cast serious doubts on the ability of provinces to perform the functions assigned to them by the central government. The People's Assembly Committee that evaluated the results of devolution during the 1970s was blunt in its conclusions: "It became apparent that the insufficiency of funds was the basic cause of weaknesses in the institutions of the People's Local Government and of turning them into empty skeletons," the committee (Democratic Republic of the Sudan 1976, p. 38) reported. "It also killed any ambitions or hope for developing current services, let alone for presenting new services to the people."

A detailed study of decentralization in Southern Darfur Province of the Sudan stressed the financial problems of the provinces and their impacts on decentralized administration. The survey revealed that the amounts of financial resources transferred to the province through the budget were far below the minimum amounts needed to implement functions transferred from the central ministries. The Ministry of Finance cut the budgets requested by the province executive councils by 50 percent in some years. The provinces were never reimbursed for minor public works expenditures made during previous fiscal years. At the same time, the central government increased the amounts that the provinces would have to collect in local taxes to levels far beyond their capacity. The result was a severe shortfall in revenues that constrained the executive council's ability to provide services or undertake development projects (Davey 1976, 38).

In much of the Sudan, as in other developing countries, the revenue base is simply too small to provide adequate tax resources. The forms of taxation that can be imposed on subsistence economies are extremely limited. In the Sudan they consisted primarily of personal property taxes that were difficult to assess and collect. In much of the country, local revenues were derived from nonproductive personal property levies--herd, date tree, and land taxes--that can be traced back to ancient times. Recording, auditing, and tax collection were often so expensive in relation to the amounts collected that revenue raising was unrewarding for many local councils. The problems were even more serious among nomadic groups (World Bank 1979).

Shortages of skilled personnel and financial resources have also undermined decentralization in Latin America. Because they lack financial resources, local governments have difficulty covering their basic operating expenses, training their personnel, purchasing equipment, making organizational improvements, obtaining technical assistance, and expanding the range and quality of public services. Harris (1983) notes: "Their limited funds make it impossible for them to improve their administrative capacity. And their limited administrative capacity discourages the allocation of new functions, for fear that they will not be able to carry them out effectively or use the funds given to them efficiently. Finally, their limited administrative capacity greatly hinders their ability to levy and collect taxes or mobilize their own sources of revenue."

Recent financial reforms in Mexico have merely deepened the problem. The federal government has attempted to strengthen the role of municipal governments by reducing its involvement in local affairs, but this effort has not improved the status of municipal governments because they have inadequate financial resources, trained personnel, and political support. Federal agencies continue to carry out the bulk of projects that provide local services and functions.

All of this leads to the conclusion that, before centralization can be pushed ahead, much more needs to be learned about local public finance. In North Africa, as in other developing regions, the dearth of solid information on local revenue generation, on local council or administrative budgeting, and on the central government's grant and loan process for subnational units, limits the discussion of decentralization to what are essentially secondary and indirect matters. The heart of the matter—money—is placed on the edge and not at the center of the discourse. It is true that what information is available indicates continuing centralization of most fiscal authority, but a consideration of where changes could be effected demands more precise and detailed information on how the present systems function. Such a study, or studies, would most likely indicate that the central grant and loan process everywhere remains of paramount importance. Yet, it would still be revealing to have precise knowledge of the strategies used by administrative subunits and councils to secure central funds.

Finally, the capacity of decentralized units to carry out their assigned responsibilities has also been adversely affected by the limited physical infrastructure and transport and communications facilities in rural areas. The lack of infrastructure and the restricted access to services and facilities in rural Tanzania, Kenya, and the Sudan, for example, has hindered interaction among local development committees, district and provincial governments, and between them and the central government. Thus, it has been difficult for central ministries to create supporting linkages. Decentralized units have found it hard to interact with each other or to coordinate their activities within regions. Relatively little attention has been given in the design and implementation of decentralization policies to the impacts of spatial and physical conditions.

Financial, human, and physical resource constraints have inhibited the successful implementation of decentralization in nearly all developing countries. The limited resources made available to local organizations in the initial stages of decentralization undermine decentralization policies and maintain weak local institutions.

VI. Conclusions and Implications

Decentralization is not a "quick fix" for the administrative, political, or economic problems of developing countries. Its application does not automatically overcome shortages of skilled personnel; in fact, initially it creates greater demand for them. Its application does not, of itself, guarantee that larger amounts of resources will be generated at the local level. Initially, decentralization may be more costly, simply because it encourages more groups, communities, and levels of administration to undertake development activities. Although decentralization has been modestly successful in a number of countries, an analysis of recent experiences does not establish definitively that reorganization was the only factor that increased production or improved administration.

The available assessments of decentralization are qualitative and episodic. They deal mainly with the social and political issues, offering little in the way of economic or quantitative analysis or hard policy prescriptions. They indicate that one form of decentralization may have worked fairly well in one country, whereas in others a similar (but never exactly the same) arrangement produced the opposite or drastically different effects. The arguments in favor of decentralization are usually a priori rationalizations based on plausibility: they posit a likelihood that positive results will occur from structural or procedural reforms.

Given the shortcomings revealed by recent experience, should attempts to decentralize be abandoned? Definitely not. As the experiences of Indonesia, Morocco, Papua New Guinea and Thailand (among others) demonstrate, much can be achieved through small-scale, incremental transfers of powers and responsibilities, especially for local management functions. Decentralization must be viewed more realistically, however, not as a general solution to all of the problems of underdevelopment, but rather as one of a range of administrative or organizational devices that may improve the efficiency, effectiveness, and responsiveness of various levels of government under suitable conditions. How do governments determine when conditions are suitable? Growing pressures to decentralize may be the best indicator. They may stem from the government's own assessment of the inadequacy of highly centralized arrangements, from the demands of local organizations and officials, from increasing regional dissidence or ethnic tension, or, not uncommonly, from fiscal and intellectual pressures from international donors. Decentralization is likely to be more effective in countries where governments have been in office for some time and where regimes are not faced with imminent social or economic crises. Such countries tend to have some reserves of resources and trained personnel to assign to decentralized programs. They are often best able to take advantage of resources made available by international donors.

Decentralization is not usually suitable for countries in deep crisis; it cannot be recommended as a last-ditch effort to avoid catastrophe (though some governments in deep crisis, such as in the Sudan, have opted for decentralization). A common-sense conclusion is that governments survive the worst phases of crises by centralizing, but that they try to avoid potentially deeper crises later by decentralizing.

As with all managerial activities, the more successful decentralization efforts are those that are thoroughly prepared and carefully implemented. Assessments of the more successful ventures lead to the following operational principles. These, it must be noted, are based on hypotheses that remain to be tested by planners of both developing countries and international assistance agencies.

1. Principle: <u>Plan small; expand incrementally</u>.

    a. Hypothesis: Small-scale decentralization programs designed for limited impact will generate more positive and durable results than large-scale, sweeping, organizational reforms.

    b. Rationale: The smaller the program, the less threatening it will be and the less demanding of resources and personnel. That small ventures are less likely to be discarded at the first disappointment, is particularly important in the light of the second operational principle, described below. Small programs are more likely to attract donors, who can see bearable costs in limited operations. Small programs are more easily controlled and evaluated and are easier to learn from and to readjust. Successful small efforts can be expanded incrementally as personnel and organizations attain greater skills and capacity to plan and manage development activities.

2. Principle: <u>Plan for the "long term."</u>

    a. Hypothesis: Decentralization requires a lengthy period of gestation before its benefits will be realized.

    b. Rationale: Decentralization is an attempt to counteract, not to reinforce, ingrained bureaucratic and managerial behavior. Its success depends in large part on changes in attitudes and behavior that have been bred by and maintained through highly centralized structures and procedures. As such, decentralization requires thorough design, analysis, and preparation, which, in turn, require a relatively long period for implementation before positive results can be seen. Because decentralization often goes against the grain of tradition and custom and against the interests of those whose support is most important for its success, it cannot be implemented without conflict. The inevitable conflicts can only be resolved through education and persuasion, processes that require a great deal of time.

3. Principle: Plan "tutorially".

   a. Hypothesis: Decentralization programs in which the first stages are closely supervised efforts to teach local staff and citizens how to handle new responsibilities will be more successful than those that transfer large numbers of tasks or great responsibility all at once.

   b. Rationale: In much of the Third World, centralist patterns and attitudes have become entrenched. Low-level officials and local groups sometimes appear incapable of seizing initiatives, even when they are legally and financially empowered to do so. In other cases, the transfer of large responsibilities to inexperienced people has resulted in drastic declines in efficiency of delivery systems and in the quality of public services. Successful programs for decentralization must break the ingrained resistance to local initiative without disrupting essential government activities. A tutorial perspective on the part of central officials is required. This involves the piecemeal, incremental building up of responsibilities and resources of decentralized institutions. This runs the risk of excessively close supervision and central paternalism, but it may be the most that circumstances will bear.

4. Principle: Plan for donor involvement, but at the same time the gradual phase-out of donor activities.

   a. Hypothesis: Programs of decentralization that use the financial and personnel resources of donors will be better planned and more easily launched than those not involving international agencies. But when developing countries rely exclusively on donors, the long-range impact of decentralization will be constrained.

   b. Rationale: Decentralization requires strong, sustained political commitment; extra resources; new patterns of administrative behavior; a reorientation of attitudes and relationships; and, indeed, a long list of other requirements. The participation of international agencies can be crucial to the successful implementation of decentralization. They can provide the means necessary to experiment and can help to persuade leaders that it is a wise and profitable course of action. Many decentralization programs in the Third World would simply never have been initiated without the involvement of international agencies. The obvious danger is the possibility of establishing a dependent relationship, in which a government relies totally on the donor and commits few or no resources to the program. Donors, of course, are aware of this problem and are eager to find ways to build "sustainability" into their projects. The mutual interests of the host government and international agencies will be served by maximizing from the outset the financial and personnel commitments of the host government to decentralization. Such programs should be supported by donors only when the host government has a substantial stake in the operation.

5. Principle: Plan for Training.

   a. Hypothesis: Decentralization programs that include a component for the training of central administrators and local staff, officials, and citizens, will be more likely to have a positive impact and to endure than those that do not.

   b. Rationale: In most countries, decentralization of any sort imposes additional (or at least different) burdens on administrators and institutions. Extra staff must usually be provided; at a minimum, existing staff and popular representatives must be informed of their new responsibilities and instructed on how to carry them out. Moreover, decentralization implies a new set of roles for central administrators, requiring less central initiation and greater facilitation of decentralized planning, decisionmaking and management. Training could help to reorient central administrators to their new tasks of supervision and support.

6. Principle: Plan on a "grant" basis.

a. Hypothesis: Decentralization policies that transfer adequate financial resources as well as powers and responsibilities will be more successful than those that merely call for consultation with or participation of local officials or citizenry.

b. Rationale: It is better to start decentralization by giving the organizations to which responsibilities are transferred money to allocate rather than rules to follow. Even when the funds are modest and the final authority remains with central agencies, the concrete tasks of allocating resources will do more to galvanize local action than even the grandest abstract discussions.

In sum, a decentralization program is more likely to succeed if it is small in scope, has a long period of time in which to prove itself, centers around specific financial functions, transfers responsibilities and authority incrementally, is sparing of donor involvement, and includes a training component. The more of these features that are built in, the better the chances that staff activity and productivity will increase, that citizen participation in government activities will expand and be meaningful, that the planned goals of projects will be more rapidly and economically achieved, and that meaningful development will occur. There can be no guarantee that these laudable ends will be reached; the most that can be said--from a reading of experience--is that these are the principles that appear to have worked.

Annex 1:

Donor Assisted Decentralization—Indonesia's Provincial Development Program (PDP)

Indonesia's Provincial Development Program was conceived in the mid 1970s and launched in 1979. Operating in ten of the country's twenty-seven provinces and serving more than 50 percent of Indonesia's population, the program has three main goals:

- To build a planning and implementing capacity at the local level.

- To rely on development projects of a sufficiently small scale that lowest level officials and local populations can actively participate in the planning and implementing processes.

- To ensure that projects benefit the rural poor in the PDP areas.

The present phase of the PDP has a total budget of about US$60 million, of which $20 million comes from the government of Indonesia. [1] The remaining $40 million comes from three international sources: the United States Agency for International Development (USAID), which has partially granted and mostly loaned Indonesia $32 million to support the PDP in eight provinces, and the International Development Association and the Federal Republic of Germany, which each support the program in a single province.

---

[1] Colin MacAndrews, "Planning from Below—The Indonesian Provincial Development Programme" (Jakarta: 1981; processed). USAID/Government of Indonesia PDP.

Each of the participating provinces is receiving $6 million, spread over a four-year period. One-sixth of this sum supports the expatriate consultant team in the province <u>and</u> training programs for Indonesian staff. The rest is allocated to designing and carrying out small development projects in such fields as rural credit, irrigation, rural industries, multicropping trials, animal husbandry improvement, training, and community development. The criteria for projects are that they focus on the rural poor, and that they have "quick payoffs," offering concrete results within a twelve month period. [2]

Special care is taken to involve the local officials and population in the identification, setting-up, running, and evaluation of projects. This task has not been easy. Indonesian civil servants have been long accustomed to top-down management in a system that has stressed national integration and political and economic stability. In its early stages, the PDP was more of an educational than a planning exercise. Eliciting the involvement of officials --much less ordinary citizens--required lengthy and repeated explanations.

A second factor hindering the PDP's progress was weak interdepartmental coordination. Even minor decisions required a formal and complicated process of consensus-building. Some of these difficulties were overcome when the PDP was based in the powerful Ministry of Home Affairs, which has authority over all levels of local government. The longer run solution to these problems is the creation of a cadre of officials with applied technical skills, who will continue to work in the local government system. Thus, the PDP is giving considerable attention to training.

---

[2] Jerome French, <u>et al</u>., "Evaluation of the Provincial Area Development Program" (USAID, September 1981;) Processed.

Available figures show that, through 1981, some 244 projects had been undertaken in four of the ten PDP provinces. PDP reports claim that all projects are reviewed annually by Indonesia's provincial planning offices, and by USAID in the eight provinces where it supports the program. Initiatives assessed as successful can be funded for a second year, replicated in suitable locales elsewhere in and outside the province, or moved to a "credit stage," where farmers borrow money to continue applying the new technique they learned in the first year. 3/

The percentage of successful projects in not known. Part of the PDP was evaluated by a USAID team in 1981, and Indonesian scholars and government officals have also reviewed the program. The overall conclusions are that the PDP clearly demonstrates Indonesia's capability to manage a diffuse project of this nature, that provincial and local government performance levels have been improved, that the PDP has had a beneficial impact on the rural poor, and that there has been a genuine involvement of local communities in the PDP. 4/

Although it is clear that the funds and support of the donors, especially USAID, have been crucial in launching the program and assisting in its success to date, it is equally obvious that the PDP is dependent on international agencies and will continue to be so for the near future. If the donors were to withdraw their assistance suddenly, the program could simply come to a halt. The government of Indonesia is deeply involved in the venture, but many of its costs are for civil service salaries, which would

---

3/ Moeljarto, Tjokrowinoto, "Small Village Credit Program of the Provincial Development Program in East Java," paper read at the United Nations Center for Regional Development, Senior Level Seminar on Implementing Decentralization Policies and Programmes. Nagoya, Japan, 1983.

4/ French, "Evaluation of the Provincial Area Development Program."

continue to be paid even if the PDP were to disappear. It is not clear that the government recognizes the PDP as important enough that it would cover costs for the other two-thirds of the project if the donors withdrew.

Thus, the task at hand is to find ways of combining donor assistance, which can be vital and helpful, with mechanisms that, <u>at the very outset of project planning</u>, aim at the eventual phasing out of donor involvement and leaving the host country with a self-sustaining effort. While self-sufficiency is highly desirable in almost all donor-assisted development projects, it is particularly important in decentralization efforts, the success or failure of which so totally depends on the level of host country government commitment. 5/

5/ Dennis A. Rondinelli, "Implementing Decentralization Programmes in Asia: A Comparative Analysis," <u>Public Administration and Development</u>, vol. 3 (1983). In press.

Annex 2:

China—The "Production Responsibility System"

In December 1978, the Central Committee of the Chinese Communist Party approved a set of resolutions designed to increase agricultural production. The resolutions, and the subsequent measures taken to implement them, constitute a significant break from China's past policy. They aim at stimulating peasant productivity by:

- Increasing the proportion of privately farmed to communally farmed land,

- Diversifying agricultural production and allowing freer rein for household sideline production,

- Expanding the role of rural markets,

- Increasing expenditure on agricultural infrastructure,

- Raising the prices paid to producers of grain and other crops while reducing the price of farm machinery and fertilizer,

- Reducing or eliminating agricultural taxes in poorer regions.

A key organizational change, called the Production Responsibility System has been introduced on the 53,000 communes in rural China. Because the essence of these innovations in general, and the Production Responsibility System in particular, is to expand the role of markets and to promote production by reducing the scope and intensity of direct government control at the level of the production unit, it is fair to classify these efforts as decentralization. Increasing low-level autonomy, while decreasing the involvement of higher level bureaucrats, is a form of deconcentration.

How does this new system work? As was the case before 1979, each commune is divided into production brigades consisting of two to three hundred households. In turn, these are divided into production teams of twenty to thirty households. At a guess, there are more than six million production teams in rural China. The system still retains many of its former centralist features--each production brigade is assigned a list of crops to produce, allotted commune land on which to produce them, and given a productivity quota per hectare.

Brigade authorities are closely consulted before these assignments are made, and a great deal of discussion and compromise is involved. Each brigade wants to make sure that it is given a fair share of high quality land and the right to grow the most profitable crops, such as vegetables for communes near an urban market. Available descriptions indicate that commune authorities (who receive their quotas from county or municipal officials) take care to see that good land and profitable assignments are equitably shared, to the point of reassigning land allotments annually, and by paying subsidies to brigades with poor land or unprofitable but necessary crop assignments.

Up to this point, the system does not appear to depart from the egalitarian emphasis of the Maoist period. The changes become visible at the level of the production team. Although these have long been important work units, the new system elevates them to focal points of the effort to stimulate agricultural production.

Previously, the production team as a whole was assigned a production quota. Members were rewarded for their labor by means of "work points." Work points were awarded on the basis of physical capacity, skills, and attitude. It was a system of equal pay for unequal work. The new system still assigns work points, but the size of the labor group has been reduced. Further, the individuals in the team are more responsible for their own scheduling of time and effort. Most important, there are now rewards for exceeding the production quotas. The crucial new feature of the Production Responsibility System is that the <u>households</u> in production teams may contract with the commune to produce a specified amount of a crop, which will be turned over to the commune at a fixed, or "quota," price. Household production over and above the quota can be sold by the household to government buyers, at a much higher "above quota price," 50 percent higher in the case of rice in the Shanghai Area in 1981, for example. 1/ The negative corollary is that households are now responsible for underproduction; those that fail to meet their normal quota must make up the difference from storage or other resources.

To illustrate, assume that Production Team x is assigned a grain quota of y. How is this quota determined? The principle is that a team's quota is its average (or perhaps the land's average--this is not clear) production for the previous three years, minus food, seed, fodder, and tax (the latter normally equivalent to 4 percent of production). This quota is normally "substantially below the actual surplus after deducting for producer's use." 2/ Moreover, the authorities normally do not change a quota for several years. What all this amounts to is a substantial reduction in the state monopoly grain quotas. For Production Team x, any grain production above amount y will receive the higher price. Estimates are that, since 1979,

---

1/ Lee Chong Yeong, "Food Marketing System in China--With Particular Reference to Shanghai Area" (Bangkok, Thailand: Regional FAO Office, Asia and Pacific, December 1981: processed), p. 3.

2/ Ibid.

many production teams that have opted for the new system are exceeding their quotas by 25-50 percent. 3/

There is widespread agreement that substantial agricultural production increases have taken place in China since 1979, especially in grains, cotton, oils, and sugar. The production increases have been accompanied by increases in the net incomes of peasants--from an average of 115 yuan in 1978 to 200 yuan in 1981. 4/ Recent observers say that more is being produced, there is more to eat, and cash incomes are higher. The popularity of the new system is indicated by the fact that 80 percent of all production teams have opted for the new system, though it is not compulsory. 5/

Within the production team the assignments of work are increasingly made to individuals or households, not to groups. Individuals are no longer required to work even the collective land on a group basis, but many come and go according to their own personal work schedule. It appears that households can rent or buy machinery, fertilizer, and other resources of the commune for their own private plot production. None of the available documents mention the hiring of labor, and it seems very likely that this is still forbidden.

A second source of increased production is the increase in the size of allowable private plots (now 130 m2 for a family of four), and the freedom to sell all produce from private plots on "free" markets. (The quotation

---

3/ Ibid.

4/ Ma Gengou, "The Responsibility System of Agricultural Production in China." Paper read at United Nations Center for Regional Development Senior Level Seminar on Implementing Decentralization Policies and Programmes, Nagoya, Japan August 1982.

5/ Ibid.

marks are necessary because price ceilings for products are often set by official market regulators.) Prices for produce in the open market are higher than those in the state-run distribution network. But the quality of produce is said to be demonstrably higher, and there are no waiting lines. Barring a dramatic reversal of offical policy and ideology, it would seem that the impact of privatization will be increased, as the "Chinese agricultural bank (has) started to provide production loans to individual farmers to cultivate private plots." 6/ But, of course, dramatic policy reversals cannot be ruled out in China. Indeed, one observer notes that Chinese peasants certainly approve of the new system, but openly wonder whether it will last. 7/

The Chinese authorities insist that they are using the market mechanism, the expansion of private plots, and the Production Responsibility System as production-enhacing devices, not to eliminate but "to supplement the planned economy." 8/ They point out that an overwhelming percentage of land is still owned collectively. The division of commune land between and among brigades and teams is still conducted annually. Central directives and controls are still of great importance. Prices are still regulated. On the other hand, it is acknowledged that "income disparities between Production Teams have increased" 9/ since the introduction of the new system. China is beginning to move away from strict egalitarianism in order to stimulate

---

6/ Yeong, "Food Marketing System in China," p. 14.

7/ Ibid.

8/ Ibid., p. 16.

9/ G. Shabbir Cheema, "Decentralization and Rural Development--The Case Study of Qi-Yi People's Commune in China" (Nagoya, Japan: 1982; processed), p. 31.

production. The Chinese, too, must deal with the tradeoff between equity and efficiency, and they are finding that modest decentralization of production activities can have significant results.

Annex 3:

Decentralization--The Programme de Developpement Rural in Tunisia

In 1973, the Government of Tunisia established a Rural Development Program (Programme de developpement rural--PDR). This effort, essentially a grant activity, has now had almost a decade of modestly successful operation. It works as follows: Each of Tunisia's twenty gouvernorats (administrative divisions roughly equivalent to a province; of normally quite limited autonomy) receive annually a set sum, at present about US$1.75 million. The generally poorer noncoastal gouvernorats receive $3.5 million. These funds must be spent on locally generated and supervised projects: those that promote community development and employment tend to be favored. Gouvernorate-level civil servants are charged with the tasks of identifying projects, studying their feasibility and potential payoff, harmonizing the proposed action with nationally conceived operations in the region, and supervising implementation.

Though small, the PDR has proved significant. Officials can respond quickly and flexibly to local opportunities and local crises. The generally large number of demands on the very limited funds has its positive side: gouvernorat officials have been forced to learn how to justify projects on the basis of the quality of the investment vis-a-vis nationally set guidelines. Various internal government reviews of the PDR have all been positive. The sums available under the program have been increased, and the smooth operation of the PDR has been cited as one justification for the more far-reaching decentralization and regional planning proposals now under consideration in Tunisia.

All projects proposed must be put forward according to a detailed schedule imposed by the central Ministry of Plan, and all projects must be approved by Tunis before funds can be spent. Tunisian informants state that this is not a pro forma vetting operation; projects can be and have been turned down. Given the central officials' close control of the program, it is clear that the PDR is but a limited measure of deconcentration. The government of Tunisia offers the view that the capacities of its local staff are for the moment somewhat limited; thus one must start small, with a closely supervised effort. In the normally highly centralized Tunisian context, the PDR was, and is, a significant first step toward greater decentralization.

References

Ali, A., and H. Gunasekera. "Implementing Decentralization Policies and Programmes: The Case of Fiji." Paper read at United Nations Center for Regional Development Senior Level Seminar, Nagoya, Japan, August 1982.

American Public Health Association. Community Financing of Primary Health Care. Washington, D.C., 1982.

Apthorpe, R. "Peasants and Planistrators: Rural Cooperatives in Tunisia." The Magreb Review, vol. 2, no. 1 (January/February, 1977).

Berry R., and R. Jackson. "Interprovincial Inequalities and Decentralization in Papua New Guinea." Third World Planning Review, vol. 3, no. 1 (1981): 57-76.

Boodhoo, M. "The Organization and Management of Development Agencies: A Comparative Perspective." International Review of Administrative Sciences, 42 (1976): 221-236.

Cheema, G.S. "The Organization and Management of Public Enterprises for Regional Development in Asia." Public Enterprise, vol. 2, no. 4 (1982): 21-36.

_____. "The Role of Voluntary Organizations in Decentralized Development." In Decentralization and Development: Policy Implementation in Developing Countries. Edited by G. S. Cheema and D. A. Rondinelli. Beverly Hills: Sage, 1983.

Cheema, G. S. and D. A. Rondinelli, Eds. Decentralization and Development. Beverly Hills: Sage, 1983.

Conyers, D. "Papua New Guinea: Decentralization and Development from the Middle." In Development from Above or Below? Edited by W. Stohr and D.R.F. Taylor. London: Wiley, 1981.

Conyers, D., and R. Westcott. "Regionalism in Papua New Guinea." Administration for Development, 13 (1979): 1-28.

Cuca, R., and C. Pierce. Experiments in Family Planning: Lessons from the Developing World. Baltimore: Johns Hopkins University Press, 1977.

Davey, K., ed. Local Government and Development in the Sudan: The Experience in Southern Darfur Province. Khartoum: Academy of Administrative and Professional Sciences, Ministry of People's Local Government, 1976.

El Bashir, M. "Bureaucracy and Development: General Impressions of the Sudanese Experience." African Administrative Studies, 16 (1976): 21-25.

Ergas, Z. "Why Did Ujamaa Village Policy Fail? Towards a Global Analysis." Journal of Modern African Studies, vol. 18, no. 3 (1980): 387-410.

Esman, M., and J. Montgomery. "The Administration of Human Development." Implementing Programs of Human Development. Edited by P.T. Knight. World Bank Staff Working Paper no. 403. Washington, D.C., 1982.

Fabrikant, R. "Developing Country State Enterprise: Performance and Control." Columbia Journal of Transnational Law, vol. 15, no. 1 (1975): 40-56.

Friedman, H. "Local Political Alternatives for Decentralized Development." In Decentralization and Development: Policy Implementation in Developing Countries. Edited by G.S. Cheema and D.A. Rondinelli. Beverly Hills: Sage, 1983.

Gengou, M. "Responsibility System of Agricultural Production in China." Paper read at United Nations Center for Regional Development Senior Level Seminar on Implementing Decentralization Policies and Programmes, Nagoya, Japan, 1982.

Graham, L. "Latin America." International Handbook on Local Government Reorganization. Edited by D. Rowat. Westport, Conn.: Greenwood Press, 1980.

Hallet, E. "Joint Ventures in Developing Countries." In Private Foreign Investment and the Developing World. Edited by P. Ady. New York: Praeger, 1971.

Harris, R. "Centralization and Decentralization in Latin America." In Decentralization and Development: Policy Implementation in Developing Countries. Edited by G.S. Cheema and D.A. Rondinelli. Beverly Hills: Sage, 1983.

Hinchliffe, K. "Conflicts Between National Aims in Papua New Guinea: The Case of Decentralization and Equality." Economic Development and Cultural Change, vol. 28, no. 4 (1980): 819-38.

Hyden, G. "Administration and Public Policy." In Politics and Public Policy in Kenya and Tanzania. Edited by J. Barkan and J. Okumu. New York: Praeger, 1976.

Idode, J. "Nigeria." In International Handbook on Local Government Reorganization. Edited by D. Rowat. Westport, Conn.: Greenwood Press, 1980.

Iglesias, G. "Political and Administrative Issues in Regional Planning and Development." Philippine Journal of Public Administration, vol. XXI, nos. 3 and 4 (1977): 324-341.

James, E. "The Nonprofit Sector in International Perspective: The Case of Sri Lanka." Journal of Comparative Economics, vol. 6, no. 2 (1982): 99-129.

Khalil, H. "The Sudan Gezira Scheme: Some Institutional and Administrative Aspects." Journal of Administration Overseas, vol. 9, no. 4 (1970): 273-85.

Khan, D. A. "Implementing Decentralization Policies and Programmes: A Case Study of the Integrated Rural Development Programme in Punjab, Pakistan." Paper read at United Nations Center for Regional Development Senior Level Seminar on Implementing Decentralization Policies and Programmes, Nagoya, Japan.

King, J. Economic Development Projects and Their Appraisal. Baltimore: Johns Hopkins University Press, 1967.

Kjekshus, H. "The Tanzanian Villagization Policy: Implementation Lessons and Ecological Dimensions." Canadian Journal of African Studies, vol. XI, no. 2 (1977): 269-82.

Kolawole, A. "The Role of Grassroots Participation in National Development: Lessons from the Kwara State of Nigeria." Community Development Journal, vol 17, no. 2 (1982): 121-33.

Korten, F. "Community Participation: A Management Perspective on Obstacles and Options." In Bureaucracy and the Poor: Closing the Gap. Edited by D. C. Korten and F. B. Alfonso. Singapore: McGraw-Hill, 1981. pp. 181-221.

Lamb, G. "Market Surrogate Approaches to Institutional Development." Washington, D.C.: The World Bank, 1982. Processed.

Landau, M. Final Report: Provincial Development Assistant Program, Philippines. Berkeley: Project on Managing Decentralization, Institute of International Studies, University of California, 1980.

Lele, U. The Design of Rural Development: Lessons from Africa. Baltimore: Johns Hopkins University Press, 1975.

Leonard, D. Reaching the Peasant Farmer: Organization Theory and Practice in Kenya. Chicago: University of Chicago Press, 1977.

_____. "Interorganizational Linkages for Decentralized Rural Development: Overcoming Administrative Weaknesses." In Decentralization and Development: Policy Implementation in Developing Countries. Edited by G. S. Cheema and D. A. Rondinelli. Beverly Hills: Sage, 1983.

MacAndrews, C., A. Sibero, and H. Fisher. "Regional Development, Planning and Implementation in Indonesia: The Evolution of a National Policy." Paper read at United Nations Center for Region Development Seminar on Rural Development, Nagoya, Japan, 1981.

Maddick, H. Democracy, Decentralization and Development. Bombay: Asia Publishing House, 1963.

Mathur, K. "Small Farmers Development Agency in India: An Experiment in Controlled Decentralization." Paper read at United Nations Center for Regional Development Senior Level Seminar on Implementing Decentralization Policies and Programmes, Nagoya, Japan, 1982.

Mbithi, P., and C. Barnes. *A Conceptual Analysis of Approaches to Rural Development.* Discussion Paper No. 204. Nairobi: University of Nairobi, Institute of Development Studies, 1975.

Moeljarto, Tjokrowinoto. "Small Village Credit Program of the Provincial Development Program in East Java." Paper read at United Nations Center for Regional Development Senior Level Seminar on Implementing Decentralization Policies and Programmes, Nagoya, Japan, 1982.

Montgomery, J. "Allocation of Authority in Land Reform Programs: A Comparative Study of Administrative Processes and Outputs." *Administrative Science Quarterly*, 17 (1972): 62-75.

Moris, J. "The Transferability of Western Management Concepts and Programs: An East African Perspective." In *Education and Training for Public Sector Management in Developing Countries.* Edited by D. Stifel, J. S. Coleman, and J. E. Black. New York: Rockefeller Foundation, 1976.

Nellis, J. "Three Aspects of the Kenyan Administrative System." *Cultures at Developpement*, 5 (1973): 541-70.

_____. "Decentralization in North Africa: Problems of Policy Implementation." In *Decentralization and Development: Policy Implementation in Developing Countries.* Edited by G. S. Cheema and D. A. Rondinelli. Beverly Hills: Sage, 1983.

_____. "Tutorial Decentralization: The Case of Morocco." Working Paper. Syracuse: Syracuse University Graduate Program in Development Planning, 1983b.

Nor Abdul Ghani, M. "Management of Decentralization: A Case Study of the Federal Agricultural Marketing Authority (FAMA) in Malaysia." Paper read at United Nations Center for Regional Development Senior Level Seminar on Implementing Decentralization Policies and Programmes, Nagoya, Japan, 1982.

Noranitipadungkarn, C. "Creating Local Capacity for Development Through Decentralization Programmes in Thailand." Paper read at United Nations Center for Regional Development Senior Level Seminar on Implementing Decentralization Policies and Programmes, Nagoya, Japan, 1982.

Okafor, F. "Community Involvement in Rural Development: A Field Study in the Bendel State of Nigeria." *Community Development Journal*, vol. 17, no. 2 (1982): 134-40.

Ralston, L., J. Anderson, and E. Colson. *Voluntary Efforts in Decentralized Management.* Berkeley: University of California, Program on Managing Decentralization, Institute of International Studies, 1981.

Rondinelli, D. "National Investment Planning and Equity Policy in Developing Countries: The Challenge of Decentralized Administration." *Policy Sciences*, vol. 10, no. 1 (1978): 45-74.

_____. *Administrative Decentralization and Area Development Planning in East Africa: Implications for U.S. Aid Policy*. Madison: University of Wisconsin Regional Planning and Area Development Project, 1980.

_____. "Government Decentralization in Comparative Perspective: Theory and Practice in Developing Countries." *International Review of Administrative Science*, vol. 47, no. 2 (1981a): 133-45.

_____. "Administrative Decentralization and Economic Development: The Sudan's Experience with Devolution." *Journal of Modern African Studies*, vol. 19, no. 4 (1981b): 595-624.

_____. "Implementation of Decentralization Programs in Asia: A Comparative Analysis." *Public Administration and Development*, vol. 3 (1983). (In press)

Royaume de Maroc. *Project de Plan de Developpement Economique et Social*. Rabat: Government Printer, 1981.

Sherwood, F. "Devolution as a Problem of Organization Strategy." In *Comparative Urban Research*. Edited by R.T. Daland. Beverly Hills: Sage, 1969.

Streeten, P. "New Approaches to Private Overseas Investment." In *Private Foreign Investment and the Developing World*. Edited by P. Ady. New York: Praeger, 1971.

Sudan, Democratic Republic of. *Final Report of the Select Committee for Study and Revision of the People's Local Government*. Khartoum: People's Assembly, 1976.

Tordoff, W. "Ghana." In *International Handbook on Local Government Reorganization*. Edited by D. Rowat. Westport, Conn.: Greenwood Press, 1980.

United Nations. *Changes and Trends in Public Administration and Finance for Development--Second Survey, 1977-1979*. New York: United Nations Department of Technical Cooperation for Development, ST/ESA/SERE 27, 1982.

United States Agency for International Development. *Managing Decentralization*. Project Paper. Washington, D.C., 1979a.

_____. *Country Development Strategy Statement: Kenya, 1980-1984*. Washington, D.C., 1979b.

Uphoff, N., and M. Esman. *Local Organization for Rural Development in Asia*. Ithaca: Cornell University Center for International Studies, 1974.

Vieira, P. *Toward a Theory of Decentralization: A Comparative View of Forty-Five Countries*. Ph.D. dissertation. University of Southern California, Los Angeles, 1967.

von Freyhold, M. "The Problems of Rural Development and the Politics of Ujamaa Viijini in Handeni." The African Review, vol. 6, no. 2 (1976): 36-64.

Wanasinghe, S. "Implementing Decentralization Policies and Programs: The Sri Lankan Experience." Paper read at United Nations Center on Regional Development at Senior Level Seminar on Implementing Decentralization Policies and Programmes, Nagoya, Japan, 1982.

World Bank. Sudan: Agricultural Sector Survey, vol. III. Washington, D.C., 1979.

_____. Papua New Guinea: Selected Development Issues. Washington, D.C., 1982.

World Bank Publications of Related Interest

Accelerated Development in Sub-Saharan Africa: An Agenda for Action

In the fall of 1979, the African Governors of the World Bank addressed a memorandum to the Bank's president expressing their alarm at the dim economic prospects for the nations of sub-Saharan Africa and asking that the Bank prepare a "special paper on the economic development problems of these countries" and an appropriate program for helping them. This report, building on the *Lagos Plan of Action*, is the response to that request.

The report discusses the factors that explain slow economic growth in Africa in the recent past, analyzes policy changes and program orientations needed to promote faster growth, and concludes with a set of recommendations to donors, including the recommendation that aid to Africa should double in real terms to bring about renewed African development and growth in the 1980s. The report's agenda for action is general; it indicates broad policy and program directions, overall priorities for action, and key areas for donor attention. Like the *Lagos Plan*, the report recognizes that Africa has enormous economic potential, which awaits fuller development.

1981; 2nd printing 1982. 198 pages (including statistical annex, bibliography).

French: Le développement accéléré en afrique au sud du Sahara: programme indicatif d'action.

Stock Nos. SA-1981-E, SA-1981-F. Free of charge.

The Design of Development
Jan Tinbergen

Formulates a coherent government policy to further development objectives and outlines methods to stimulate private investments.

The Johns Hopkins University Press, 1958; 6th printing, 1966. 108 pages (including 4 annexes, index).

LC 58-9458. ISBN 0-8018-0633-X, $5.00 (£3.00) paperback.

Development Strategies in Semi-Industrial Economies
Bela Balassa

Provides an analysis of development strategies in semi-industrial economies that have established an industrial base. Endeavors to quantify the systems of incentives that are applied in six semi-industrial developing economies—Argentina, Colombia, Israel, Korea, Singapore, and Taiwan—and to indicate the effects of these systems on the allocation of resources, international trade, and economic growth.

The Johns Hopkins University Press, 1982. 416 pages (including appendixes, index).
LC 81-15558. ISBN 0-8018-2569-5, $39.95 hardcover.

Eastern and Southern Africa: Past Trends and Future Prospects
Ravi Gulhati

World Bank Staff Working Paper No. 413. August 1980. 24 pages.

Stock No. WP-0413. $3.00.

Economic Development Projects and Their Appraisal: Cases and Principles from the Experience of the World Bank
John A. King

The English-language edition is out of print.

French: Projets de développement économique et leur évaluation. *Dunod Editeur, 24–26, boulevard de l'Hôpital, 75005 Paris, France. 1969.*

99 francs.

Spanish: La evaluacion de proyectors de desarrollo económico. *Editorial Tecnos, 1970. 545 pages (including indexes).*

800 pesetas.

Economic Growth and Human Resources
Norman Hicks, assisted by Jahangir Boroumand

World Bank Staff Working Paper No. 408. July 1980. iv + 36 pages (including 3 appendixes, bibliography, and references).

Stock No. WP-0408. $3.00.

NEW

The Extent of Poverty in Latin America
Oscar Altimir

This work originated in a research project for the measurement and analysis of income distribution in the Latin American countries, undertaken jointly by the Economic Commission for Latin America and the World Bank. Presents estimates of the extent of absolute poverty for ten Latin American countries and for the region as a whole in the 1970s.

World Bank Staff Working Paper No. 522. 1982. 117 pages.

ISBN 0-8213-0012-1. $5.00.

First Things First: Meeting Basic Human Needs in the Developing Countries
Paul Streeten, with
Shahid Javed Burki,
Mahbub ul Haq,
Norman Hicks,
and Frances Stewart

The basic needs approach to economic development is one way of helping the poor emerge from their poverty. It enables them to earn or obtain the necessities for life—nutrition, housing, water and sanitation, education, and health—and thus to increase their productivity.

This book answers the critics of the basic needs approach, views this approach as a logical step in the evolution of economic analysis and development policy, and presents a clearsighted interpretation of the issues. Based on the actual experience of various countries—their successes and failures—the book is a distillation of World Bank studies of the operational implications of meeting basic needs. It also discusses the presumed conflict between economic growth and basic needs, the relation between the New International Economic Order and basic needs, and the relation between human rights and basic needs.

Oxford University Press, 1981; 2nd paperback printing, 1982. 224 pages (including appendix, bibliography, index).

LC 81-16836. ISBN 0-19-520-368-2, $18.95 hardcover; ISBN 0-19-520-369-0, $7.95 paperback.

The Hungarian Economic Reform, 1968–81
Bela Balassa

Reviews the Hungarian experience with the economic reform introduced in 1968 and provides a short description of the antecedents of the reform. Analyzes specific reform measures concerning agriculture, decisionmaking by industrial firms, price determination, the exchange rate, export subsidies, import protection, and investment decisions and indicates their effects on the economy. Also examines the economic effects of tendencies toward recentralization in the 1970s, as well as recent policy measures aimed at reversing these tendencies.

World Bank Staff Working Paper No. 506. February 1982. 31 pages (including references).

Stock No. WP-0506. $3.00.

Implementing Programs of Human Development
Edited by Peter T. Knight; prepared by Nat J. Colletta, Jacob Meerman, and others.

World Bank Staff Working Paper No. 403. July 1980. iv + 372 pages (including references).

Stock No. WP-0403. $15.00.

International Technology Transfer: Issues and Policy Options
Frances Stewart

World Bank Staff Working Paper No. 344. July 1979. xii + 166 pages (including references).

Stock No. WP-0344. $5.00.

Levels of Poverty: Policy and Change
Amartya Sen

World Bank Staff Working Paper No. 401. July 1980. 91 pages (including references).

Stock No. WP-0401. $3.00.

Models of Growth and Distribution for Brazil
Lance Taylor, Edmar L. Bacha, Eliana Cardoso, and Frank J. Lysy

Explores the Brazilian experience from the point of view of political economy and computable general equilibrium income distribution models.

Oxford University Press, 1980. 368 pages (including references, appendixes, index).

LC 80-13786. ISBN 0-19-520206-6, $27.50 hardcover; ISBN 0-19-520207-4, $14.95 paperback.

Patterns of Development, 1950-1970
Hollis Chenery and Moises Syrquin

A comprehensive interpretation of the structural changes that accompany the growth of developing countries, using cross-section and time-series analysis to study the stability of observed patterns and the nature of time trends.

Oxford University Press, 1975; 3rd paperback printing, 1980. 250 pages (including technical appendix, statistical appendix, bibliography, index).

LC 74-29172. ISBN 0-19-920075-0, $19.95 hardcover; ISBN 0-19-920076-9, $8.95 paperback.

Spanish: La estructura del crecimiento ecónomico: un analisis para el período 1950–1970. Editorial Teconos, 1978.

ISBN 84-309-0741-6, 615 pesetas.

Poverty and Basic Needs Series

A series of booklets prepared by the staff of the World Bank on the subject of basic needs. The series includes general studies that explore the concept of basic needs, country case studies, and sectoral studies.

Brazil
Peter T. Knight and Ricardo J. Moran

An edited and updated edition of the more detailed publication, *Brazil: Human Resources Special Report* (see description under *Country Studies* listing).

December 1981. 98 pages (including statistical appendix, map). English.

Stock No. BN-8103. $5.00.

Malnourished People: A Policy View
Alan Berg

Discusses the importance of adequate nutrition as an objective, as well as a means of economic development. Outlines the many facets of the nutrition problem and shows how efforts to improve nutrition can help alleviate much of the human and economic waste in the developing world.

June 1981. 108 pages (including 6 appendixes, notes). English. French and Spanish (forthcoming).

Stock Nos. BN-8104-E, BN-8104-F, BN-8104-S. $5.00.

Meeting Basic Needs: An Overview
Mahbub ul Haq and Shahid Javed Burki

Presents a summary of the main findings of studies undertaken in the World Bank as part of a program for reducing absolute poverty and meeting basic needs.

September 1980. 28 pages (including 2 annexes). English, French, Spanish, Japanese, and Arabic.

Stock Nos. BN-8001-E, BN-8001-F, BN-8001-S, BN-8001-J, BN-8001-A. $3.00 paperback.

Shelter
Anthony A. Churchill

Defines the elements that constitute shelter; discusses the difficulties encountered in developing shelter programs for the poor; estimates orders of magnitude of shelter needs for the next twenty years; and proposes a strategy for meeting those needs.

September 1980. 39 pages. English, French, and Spanish.

Stock Nos. BN-8002-E, BN-8002-F, BN-8002-S. $3.00 paperback.

Water Supply and Waste Disposal

Discusses the size of the problem of meeting basic needs in water supply and waste disposal and its significance to development in the context of the International Drinking Water Supply and Sanitation Decade. Examines the Bank's past role in improving water supply and waste disposal facilities in developing countries and draws conclusions for the future.

September 1980. 46 pages. English, French, Spanish, and Arabic.

Stock Nos. BN-8003-E, BN-8003-F, BN-8003-S, BN-8003-A. $3.00 paperback.

Poverty and the Development of Human Resources: Regional Perspective
Willem Bussink, David Davies, Roger Grawe, Basil Kavalsky, and Guy P. Pfeffermann

World Bank Staff Working Paper No. 406. July 1980. iii + 197 pages (including 7 tables, 2 appendixes, references, footnotes).

Stock No. WP-0406. $5.00.

NEW

Poverty and Human Development
Paul Isenman and others

Since economic growth alone has not reduced absolute poverty, it has been necessary to consider other strategies. The strategy examined in this study — human development — epitomizes the idea that poor people should be helped to help themselves.

Four chapters provide an overview of alternative strategies; a detailed look at health, education, nutrition, and fertility; lessons from existing programs; and an examination of broader issues in planning.

Oxford University Press. 1982. 96 pages (including statistical appendix).

LC 82-2153. ISBN 0-19-520389-5, $7.95 paperback.

NEW

Reforming the New Economic Mechanism in Hungary
Bela Balassa

Evaluates the reform measures taken in 1980 and 1981 (price setting, the exchange rate and protection, wage determination and personal incomes, investment decisions, and the organizational structure) that aim at the further development of the Hungarian New Economic Mechanism, introduced on January 1, 1968.

World Bank Staff Working Paper No. 534. 1982. 56 pages.

ISBN 0-8213-0048-2. $3.00.

NEW

Social Infrastructure and Services in Zimbabwe
Rashid Faruqee

The black majority government of Zimbabwe, coming to power after a long struggle for independence, has announced its strong commitment to social services to benefit the vast majority of the population. This paper looks at issues related to education, health, housing, and other important sectors and reviews specific plans and resource requirements to help improve the standard of living of the population.

World Bank Staff Working Paper No. 495. October 1981. 111 pages (including bibliography, map).

Stock No. WP-0495. $5.00.

Structural Change and Development Policy
Hollis Chenery

A retrospective look at Chenery's thought and writing over the past two decades and an extension of his work in *Redistribution with Growth* and *Patterns of Development.* Develops a set of techniques for analyzing structural changes and applies them to some major problems of developing countries today.

Oxford University Press, 1979; 2nd paperback printing, 1982. 544 pages (including references, index).

LC 79-18026. ISBN 0-19-520094-2, $34.50 hardcover; ISBN 0-19-520095-0, $12.95 paperback.

French: Changement des structures et politique de développement. *Economica, 1981.*

ISBN 2-7178-0404-8, 80 francs.

Spanish: Cambio estructural y política de desarrollo. *Editorial Tecnos, 1980.*

ISBN 84-309-0845-5, 1,000 pesetas.

Tourism—Passport to Development? Perspectives on the Social and Cultural Effects of Tourism in Developing Countries
Emanuel de Kadt, editor

The first serious effort at dealing with the effects of tourism development in a broad sense, concentrating on social and cultural questions.

A joint World Bank–Unesco study. Oxford University Press, 1979. 378 pages (including maps, index).

LC 79-18116. ISBN 0-19-520149-3, $24.95 hardcover; ISBN 0-19-520150-7, $9.95 paperback.

French: Le tourisme—passport pour le développement: regards sur les effets socioculturels du tourisme dans les pays en voie de développement. Economica, 1980.

49 francs.

NEW

Tribal Peoples and Economic Development: Human Ecologic Considerations
Robert Goodland

At the current time, approximately 200 million tribal people live in all regions of the world and number among the poorest of the poor. This paper describes the problems associated with the development process as it affects tribal peoples; it outlines the requisites for meeting the human ecologic needs of tribal peoples; and presents general principles that are designed to assist the Banks staff and project designers in incorporating appropriate procedures to ensure the survival of tribal peoples and to assist with their development.

May 1982. vii + 111 pages (including 7 annexes, bibliography).

ISBN 0-8213-0010-5. $5.00.

The Tropics and Economic Development: A Provocative Inquiry into the Poverty of Nations
Andrew M. Kamarck

Examines major characteristics of the tropical climates that are significant to economic development.

The Johns Hopkins University Press, 1976; 2nd printing, 1979. 128 pages (including maps, bibliography, index).

LC 76-17242. ISBN 0-8018-1891-5, $11.00 (£7.75) hardcover; ISBN 0-8018-1903-2, $5.00 (£3.50) paperback.

French: Les tropiques et le développement économique: un regard sans complaisance sur la pauvreté des nations. *Economica, 1978.*

ISBN 2-7178-0110-3, 25 francs.

Spanish: Los trópicos y desarrollo económico: reflexiones sobre la pobreza de las naciones. *Editorial Tecnos, 1978.*

ISBN 84-309-0740-8, 350 pesetas.

Twenty-five Years of Economic Development, 1950 to 1975
David Morawetz

A broad assessment of development efforts shows that, although the developing countries have been remarkably successful in achieving growth, the distribution of its benefits among and within countries has been less satisfactory.

The Johns Hopkins University Press, 1977; 3rd printing, 1981. 136 pages (including statistical appendix, references).

LC 77-17243. ISBN 0-8018-2134-7, $16.50 (£8.00) hardcover;
ISBN 0-8018-2092-8, $7.95 (£3.75) paperback.

French: Vingt-cinq années de développement économique: 1950 à 1975. Economica, 1978.

ISBN 2-7178-0038-7, 26 francs.

Spanish: Veinticinco años de desarrollo económico: 1950 a 1975. Editorial Tecnos, 1978.

ISBN 84-309-0792-0, 350 pesetas.

World Development Report

A large-format series of annual studies of about 200 pages, the *World Development Report*, since its inception, has been what *The Guardian* has called "a most remarkable publication. It is the nearest thing to having an annual report on the present state of the planet and the people who live on it." Each issue brings not only an overview of the state of development, but also a detailed analysis of such topics as structural change, the varying experiences of low- and middle-income countries, the relation of poverty and human resource development, global and national adjustment, and agriculture and food stability. Each contains a statistical annex, World Development Indicators, that provides profiles of more than 120 countries in twenty-five multipage tables. The data cover such subjects as demography, industry, trade, energy, finance, and development assistance and such measures of social conditions as education, health, and nutrition.

World Development Report 1982 *(See* Publications of Particular Interest *for description and sales information.)*

World Development Report 1981 *(Discusses adjustment—global and national—to promote sustainable growth in the changing world economy.)*

World Development Report 1980 *(Discusses adjustment and growth in the 1980s and poverty and human development.)*

World Development Report 1979 *(Discusses development prospects and international policy issues, structural change, and country development experience and issues.)*

World Development Report 1978 *(Disusses the development experience, 1950–75, development priorities in the middle-income developing countries, and prospects for alleviating poverty.)*

REPRINTS

Basic Needs: The Case of Sri Lanka
Paul Isenman

World Bank Reprint Series: Number 197. Reprinted from World Development. *vol. 8 (1980): 237-58.*
Stock No. RP-0197. Free of charge.

Brazilian Socioeconomic Development: Issues for the Eighties
Peter T. Knight

World Bank Reprint Series: Number 203. Reprinted from World Development. *vol. 9, no. 11/12 (1981):1063-82.*
Stock No. RP-0203. Free of charge.

Indigenous Anthropologists and Development-Oriented Research
Michael M. Cernea

World Bank Reprint Series: Number 208. Reprinted from Indigenous Anthropology in Non-Western Countries. *edited by Hussein Fahim (Durham, North Carolina: Carolina Academic Press, 1982):121-37.*
Stock No. RP-0208. Free of charge.

Latin America and the Caribbean: Economic Performance and Policies
Guy P. Pfeffermann

World Bank Reprint Series: Number 228. Reprinted from The Southwestern Review of Management and Economics. *vol. 2, no. 1 (Winter 1982):129-72.*
Stock No. RP-0228. Free of charge.

Modernization and Development Potential of Traditional Grass Roots Peasant Organizations
Michael M. Cernea

World Bank Reprint Series: Number 215. Reprinted from Directions of Change: Modernization Theory, Research, and Realities. *Boulder, Colorado: Westview Press (1981): chapter 5.*
Stock No. RP-0215. Free of charge.

WORLD BANK PUBLICATIONS
ORDER FORM

SEND TO:
WORLD BANK PUBLICATIONS
P.O. BOX 37525
WASHINGTON, D.C. 20013
U.S.A.

or

WORLD BANK PUBLICATIONS
66, AVENUE D'IÉNA
75116 PARIS, FRANCE

Name: _____

Address: _____

_____

Stock or ISBN #	Author, Title	Qty.	Price	Total

Sub-Total Cost: _____

Postage & handling fee for more than two free items ($1.00 each): _____

Total copies: _____ Air mail surcharge ($2.00 each): _____

TOTAL PAYMENT ENCLOSED: _____

Make checks payable: WORLD BANK PUBLICATIONS

Prepayment on orders from individuals is requested. Purchase orders are accepted from booksellers, library suppliers, libraries, and institutions. All prices include cost of postage by the least expensive means. The prices and publication dates quoted in this Catalog are subject to change without notice.

No refunds will be given for items that cannot be filled. Credit will be applied towards future orders.

No more than two free publications will be provided without charge. Requests for additional copies will be filled at a charge of US $1.00 per copy to cover handling and postage costs.

Airmail delivery will require a prepayment of US $2.00 per copy.

Mail-order payment to the World Bank need not be in U.S. dollars, but the amount remitted must be at the rate of exchange on the day the order is placed. The World Bank will also accept Unesco coupons.